Violin Syllabus

2006 Edition

The Royal Conservatory of Music
Official Examination Syllabus

Introductory Level through ARCT

ISBN 1-55440-028-7

Contents

SECTION 1 — GENERAL INFORMATION

SECTION 2 — EXAMINATION REQUIREMENTS

SECTION 3 — PRACTICAL EXAMINATIONS

SECTION 4 — THEORY EXAMINATIONS

SECTION 5 — BIBLIOGRAPHY

THE SECOND CENTURY

Message from the President

The Royal Conservatory of Music was founded in 1886 with the idea that a single institution could bind the people of a nation together with the common thread of shared musical experience. More than a century later, The Royal Conservatory of Music has achieved this dream. The Royal Conservatory of Music is recognized in communities throughout North America for outstanding service to students, teachers, and parents, as well as a strict adherence to high academic standards through a variety of activities—teaching, examining, publishing, research, and community outreach.

Students and teachers benefit from a curriculum based on more than a hundred years of commitment to the highest pedagogical objectives. The strength of the curriculum is reinforced by the distinguished College of Examiners—a group of fine musicians and teachers carefully selected from across Canada, the United States, and abroad for their demonstrated skill and professionalism. A rigorous examiner apprenticeship program combined with regular evaluation procedures ensures consistency and an examination experience of the highest quality for candidates.

As you pursue your studies or teach others, you become not only an important partner with The Royal Conservatory of Music in the development of creativity, discipline, and goal setting, but also an active participant, experiencing the transcendent qualities of music itself. In a society where our day-to-day lives can become rote and routine, the human need to find self-fulfillment and to engage in creative activity has never been more necessary.

Dr. Peter C. Simon
President

Preface

The 2006 edition of the *Violin Syllabus* represents the work of dedicated teachers, performers, and examiners, whose assistance is gratefully acknowledged. This *Syllabus* replaces all previous violin syllabi, and forms the official curriculum of The Royal Conservatory of Music for violin examinations conducted by RCM Examinations.

The RCM Examinations Certificate Program for violin consists of twelve levels: an introductory level, ten graded levels (Grades 1 through 10), and an Associate of The Royal Conservatory of Music (ARCT) diploma.

Five levels of theory examinations described in the current RCM *Theory Syllabus* are designed to complement practical studies and to ensure a comprehensive knowledge and understanding of various aspects of theory. Required theory examinations begin at the Grade 5 practical level and include the following subjects: rudiments, harmony, history, counterpoint, and analysis.

RCM Examinations welcomes examination applications from all interested individuals. Applications are accepted by RCM Examinations on the understanding that candidates comply with the procedures and requirements outlined in this *Syllabus*.

For more information, please visit our website at www.rcmexaminations.org or contact:

RCM Examinations
5865 McLaughlin Road, Unit 4
Mississauga, Ontario
Canada L5R 1B8

RCM Examinations at www.rcmexaminations.org

Visit the RCM Examinations website for up-to-date information on the following topics:

- ✔ fees and dates for practical and theory examinations
- ✔ examination centres
- ✔ secondary school credit for music examinations
- ✔ RCM-authored publications
- ✔ the members of the RCM Examinations College of Examiners, with biographies
- ✔ the *Music Matters* newsletter for teachers

A number of services are also available on-line, allowing examination candidates to:

- ✔ complete and submit Examination Application Forms
- ✔ verify the receipt of examination applications
- ✔ verify the time, date, and location of examinations
- ✔ look up current examination session results
- ✔ review scans of examiners' comments for current examinations

In addition, teachers can monitor key information about their studios, including:

- ✔ daily updates on students' examination registrations
- ✔ exact dates and times of students' examinations
- ✔ convenient one-page summaries of students' results
- ✔ scanned copies of students' practical examination marking forms
- ✔ unofficial transcripts of students' complete examination histories

Section 1 – General Information

APPLICATIONS

Examination applications may be submitted or downloaded at www.rcmexaminations.org.

- Examination dates and fees for the current academic year (September 1 to August 31) are listed on the website.
- Application deadlines generally fall in early November for the winter session, in early March for the spring session, and in early June for the summer session.
- Payment for examination fees can be made by MasterCard or VISA.
- Candidates who wish to submit an application by fax or mail may download the application from the website. Payment may be made by MasterCard, VISA, cheque, or money order.

Please note that an application may not be withdrawn once it has been submitted to RCM Examinations.

EXAMINATION SCHEDULES

Examinations are typically held according to the following approximate schedule:

Practical Examinations

Winter: two weeks mid-January
Spring: first three weeks of June
Summer: two weeks mid-August

Theory Examinations

Winter: the second Friday and following Saturday in December
Spring: the second Friday and following Saturday in May
Summer: a Friday and following Saturday in mid-August

Individual examination schedules are available at www.rcmexaminations.org.

- Candidates who are unable to attend their examination must contact the local RCM Examinations Centre Representative immediately. The name of the RCM Examinations Centre Representative can be found on the candidate's examination schedule. *Please note that candidates may not exchange examination times with other candidates.*

EXAMINATION CENTRES

RCM Examinations establishes and maintains local examination centres across Canada. The location of these centres depends both on demand and on the availability of appropriate facilities. A list of examination centres is available at www.rcmexaminations.org.

A senior-level examiner will be assigned for Grade 10 and ARCT examinations. If there are insufficient senior candidates in a particular centre to warrant sending a senior-level examiner, senior candidates who have applied to be examined at that centre will be notified. Such candidates may choose to take their examination at the nearest centre where a senior-level examiner is available.

FEE EXTENSIONS AND REFUNDS

Once received by RCM Examinations, an application may not be withdrawn. No fee extensions (i.e., credit notes) or refunds are granted for candidates who fail to appear for their examinations. Fee extensions will not be granted if RCM Examinations is unable to accommodate a special request. There are no academic penalties for missed examinations.

Fee extensions or refunds will *not* be granted except under two specific conditions. Candidates who are unable to take an examination for medical reasons or because of a direct time conflict with a school examination are eligible to request *either* a fee extension for the full amount of the examination fee *or* a refund of 50 percent of their examination fee.

FEE EXTENSIONS AND REFUNDS continued

Candidates must apply in writing for fee extensions or refunds within two weeks following the examination date and submit the following documentation:

- Candidates who are unable to take an examination for *medical reasons* must submit a physician's letter along with a written request.
- Candidates who are unable to take an examination because of a *direct conflict with a school examination* must submit a letter from a school official on official letterhead along with a written request.

Fee Extensions

Fee extensions for the full amount of the examination fee are valid for *one year* from the date of the missed examination. Candidates must use their fee extension within this period. To redeem a fee extension, candidates may apply on-line at www.rcmexaminations.org to have the credit automatically applied to a new application. *Please note that fee extensions are not transferable and may not be further extended.*

Fee Refunds

Candidates who know at the time that they apply for a fee extension that they will not be able to make use of the credit within the one-year period may instead apply for a refund of 50 percent of the examination fee. *Please note that fee refunds must be requested within two weeks following the date of the missed examination.*

EXAMINATION RESULTS

Individual examination results are available at www.rcmexaminations.org.

Please note that results will not be given by telephone.

- Candidates may review a scan of the original examiner's report on-line in the "Examination Results" section of the RCM Examinations website. (Please see p. 15 for details on the grading of violin examinations.)
- Duplicate marks and transcripts are available upon written request and payment of the requisite fee.
- Teachers may review unofficial transcripts and scans of the examiners' reports for all their students on-line in the "Teacher Services" section of the RCM Examinations website.

THE EXAMINER'S EVALUATION

The examiner's written evaluation of a practical examination is intended to explain, in general terms, how the final grade was calculated and to assist the candidate in subsequent music studies.

- Examination marks reflect the examiner's evaluation of the candidate's performance during the examination.
- Examination marks do not reflect previously demonstrated abilities and skills, nor do they reflect the examiner's estimation of the candidate's potential for future development.
- Results of one examination do not in any way prejudice the candidate's results in subsequent examinations.
- Appeals on practical examinations will not be considered.

THEORY EXAMINATIONS: PREREQUISITES AND CO-REQUISITES

In order to receive a certificate or diploma for a practical examination for Grades 5 to ARCT, candidates must also complete specific RCM Examinations theory examinations.

- Theory co-requisites must be completed before or within five years after the respective session of the practical examination. *Candidates are strongly advised to complete their theoretical work before, or at the same time as, their practical examination.*
- For Grade 10 and ARCT, the five-year time limit for completion of theory co-requisites is computed from the date of the original practical examination, not from the date of any subsequent supplemental examinations.
- Candidates must complete ARCT prerequisites *before* applying for an ARCT practical examination. Candidates may not complete ARCT prerequisites in the same session in which they take the ARCT

practical examination. Teachers may review the examination histories of candidates who have taken an examination in the current academic year in the "Teacher's Services" section at www.rcmexaminations.org. This service allows teachers to confirm the completion of prerequisites and co-requisites.

- There are no *prerequisite or co-requisite* theory examinations for candidates applying for practical examinations for the Introductory Level and Grades 1 to 4.
- There are no *prerequisite* theory examinations for candidates applying for practical examinations in Grades 5 to 10.
- For more information regarding RCM Examinations theory examinations, please refer to "Theory Examinations" on p. 73 of this *Syllabus* and the current RCM *Theory Syllabus*.

Practical Certificates and Diplomas	Theory Prerequisites	Theory Co-requisites
Introductory	none	none
Grades 1 to 4	none	none
Grade 5	none	Preliminary Rudiments
Grade 6	none	Grade 1 Rudiments
Grade 7	none	Grade 2 Rudiments
Grade 8	none	Grade 2 Rudiments Introductory Harmony (optional)
Grade 9	none	Grade 2 Rudiments Grade 3 Harmony *or* Grade 3 Keyboard Harmony Grade 3 History
Grade 10	none	Grade 2 Rudiments Grade 3 History Grade 4 Harmony *or* Grade 4 Keyboard Harmony Grade 4 History
ARCT	Grade 2 Rudiments Grade 3 History Grade 4 Harmony *or* Grade 4 Keyboard Harmony Grade 4 History	Grade 4 Counterpoint Grade 5 Harmony and Counterpoint *or* Grade 5 Keyboard Harmony Grade 5 History Grade 5 Analysis

ARCT EXAMINATIONS

Candidates applying for Performer's or Teacher's ARCT examinations must have completed a Grade 10 practical examination with either a total mark of at least 75 *or* a minimum of 70 percent in each section of the practical examination. Candidates must also have completed all Grade 10 theory co-requisites with a total mark of at least 60 percent on each theory examination.

For more information regarding the Performer's ARCT examination, please refer to p. 66 of this *Syllabus*.

Teacher's ARCT Examinations

Candidates applying for the Teacher's ARCT examination are strongly advised to have at least one year of practical teaching experience.

The Teacher's ARCT Diploma will be awarded only to candidates eighteen years of age or older.

The ARCT Teacher's examination consists of three parts:

Part 1: Performance of Repertoire, Orchestral Excerpts, Technical Requirements, Ear Tests, and Sight Reading
Part 2: *Viva Voce* Examination
Part 3: Written Examination

Parts 1 and 2 constitute the practical portion of the ARCT examination and are therefore taken during a practical examination session. Part 3, a written examination, is taken during a theory examination session.

ARCT EXAMINATIONS continued

Candidates may choose to take all three parts of the Teacher's ARCT examination at one session, or they may take the parts at different sessions. The parts may be taken in any order, but all three parts must be completed within a period of two years.

Second ARCT Diplomas

The Teacher's and Performer's ARCT examinations may not be attempted at the same session.

- Candidates who have passed the Teacher's ARCT examination may obtain a Performer's diploma by taking the entire Performer's ARCT examination.
- Candidates for the Teacher's ARCT who have passed the Performer's examination will be exempt from the Repertoire and Orchestral Excerpts sections of the Teacher's ARCT practical examination. The remaining sections of the Teacher's ARCT practical examination (the Technical Requirements, Ear Tests, and Sight Reading sections of Part 1 and all of Part 2) must be taken in a single session, within five years of the date of the Performer's ARCT practical examination.

CREDITS FOR MUSICIANSHIP

Examinations in Musicianship have been developed to test a student's ability in sight singing and recognition of scales, chords, and intervals. (For more information on these examinations, please see p. 74 and the current RCM *Theory Syllabus*.) Candidates may choose to substitute their Musicianship examination mark for the Ear Test section of the Grades 8, 9, and 10, and Teacher's ARCT practical examinations. The marks will be assigned on a pro rata basis.

Musicianship	Practical Grade	Minimum Passing Mark
Junior	Grade 8	60
Intermediate	Grade 9	60
Senior	Grade 10 and Teacher's ARCT	70

- Candidates must have passed the relevant Musicianship examination at least one examination session *before* the graded practical examination.
- Candidates who wish to be exempted from the Ear Test section of their practical examination must submit both a request in writing and a photocopy of their Musicianship examination results to RCM Examinations. *Such requests must be included with the examination application.*

CERTIFICATES AND DIPLOMAS

Certificates are awarded to successful candidates in the spring and fall.

- Certificates for practical examinations in Grades 5 to 9 will be awarded once the candidate has successfully completed the theory co-requisites for the respective grade.
- Certificates for theory examinations will be awarded for each theory grade upon successful completion of *all* examinations for that theory grade.
- Grade 10 practical certificates are awarded when minimum requirements have been completed, whether or not prerequisite marks for an ARCT examination have been obtained.
- ARCT diplomas will be awarded to candidates at the annual Convocation ceremony or forwarded immediately following Convocation. Candidates may not use the designation "ARCT" before Convocation.

CERTIFICATES AND DIPLOMAS continued

Practical Certificates and Diplomas	Examinations Required
Introductory Violin	Introductory Violin
Grade 1 Violin	Grade 1 Violin
Grade 2 Violin	Grade 2 Violin
Grade 3 Violin	Grade 3 Violin
Grade 4 Violin	Grade 4 Violin
Grade 5 Violin	Grade 5 Violin, Preliminary Rudiments
Grade 6 Violin	Grade 6 Violin, Grade 1 Rudiments
Grade 7 Violin	Grade 7 Violin, Grade 2 Rudiments
Grade 8 Violin	Grade 8 Violin, Grade 2 Rudiments
Grade 9 Violin	Grade 9 Violin, Grade 2 Rudiments, Grade 3 Harmony *or* Grade 3 Keyboard Harmony, Grade 3 History
Grade 10 Violin	Grade 10 Violin, Grade 2 Rudiments, Grade 3 History, Grade 4 Harmony *or* Grade 4 Keyboard Harmony, Grade 4 History
Performer's ARCT	Performer's ARCT, Grade 2 Rudiments, Grade 3 History, Grade 4 History, Grade 4 Counterpoint, Grade 5 Harmony and Counterpoint *or* Grade 5 Keyboard Harmony, Grade 5 History, Grade 5 Analysis, Grade 6 Piano
Teacher's ARCT	Teacher's ARCT (Parts 1, 2, and 3), Grade 2 Rudiments, Grade 3 History, Grade 4 History, Grade 4 Counterpoint, Grade 5 Harmony and Counterpoint *or* Grade 5 Keyboard Harmony, Grade 5 History, Grade 5 Analysis, Grade 8 Piano
Theory Certificates	**Examinations Required**
Preliminary Rudiments	Preliminary Rudiments
Grade 1 Theory	Grade 1 Rudiments
Grade 2 Theory	Grade 2 Rudiments
Grade 3 Theory	Grade 3 Harmony *or* Grade 3 Keyboard Harmony, Grade 3 History
Grade 4 Theory	Grade 4 Harmony *or* Grade 4 Keyboard Harmony, Grade 4 History, Grade 4 Counterpoint
Grade 5 Theory	Grade 5 Harmony and Counterpoint *or* Grade 5 Keyboard Harmony, Grade 5 History, Grade 5 Analysis

SECONDARY SCHOOL MUSIC CREDITS

In many school systems, examinations from RCM Examinations are accepted as credits toward secondary school graduation diplomas. A province-by-province list of secondary school accreditation for music examinations can be found at www.rcmexaminations.org. Candidates are also advised to consult their school principal or guidance counselor about the eligibility of examinations from RCM Examinations for secondary school credit and university entrance.

REGISTERED EDUCATION SAVINGS PLAN (RESP) ELIGIBILITY

Candidates who have a Registered Education Savings Plan (RESP) may be eligible to use these funds to support private studies in music at the Grade 9, Grade 10, and ARCT levels. Please consult your RESP provider for more information.

GOLD AND SILVER MEDALS

Practical Disciplines

RCM Examinations awards Gold Medals and Silver Medals for every practical discipline. Medals are awarded on the basis of examination results. No application is required.

Gold Medals

Gold Medals are awarded for each academic year (September 1 to August 31) to both the Teacher's ARCT and the Performer's ARCT candidates who obtain the highest marks in each of the following disciplines: accordion, brass, guitar, harp, organ, percussion, piano, speech arts and drama, strings, voice, and woodwinds.

Eligibility for Gold Medals

Performer's ARCT

- Candidates must obtain a minimum of 85 percent in the practical examination, a minimum of 70 percent in *each* of the co-requisite theory examinations, and a minimum of 60 percent in the co-requisite piano examination.

Teacher's ARCT

- Candidates must obtain a minimum of 85 percent in the practical examination (Parts 1 and 2 combined), a minimum of 70 percent in the written examination (Part 3), a minimum of 70 percent in *each* of the co-requisite theory examinations, and a minimum of 60 percent in the co-requisite piano examination.
- Candidates taking the complete practical examination in one session (Parts 1 and 2 combined) and candidates taking the practical examination in two sessions (Parts 1 and 2 separately) are both eligible for the Gold Medal.
- Candidates who use the Performer's ARCT in place of the Performance of Repertoire section of the Teacher's ARCT are still eligible for the Gold Medal.

Silver Medals

Silver Medals are awarded for each academic year (September 1 to August 31) in each province or designated region to the candidates in Grades 1 to 10 who have obtained the highest marks in each grade and discipline.

- To qualify for these awards, candidates must have obtained at least 80 percent in the practical examination *and* have completed the co-requisite theory examinations for their respective grades.

Theory

A Gold Medal for Excellence in Theory will be awarded each academic year (September 1 to August 31) to the candidate who has achieved the highest *average* mark from completing all the following examinations:

Grade 3 History
Grade 4 History
Grade 5 History
Grade 3 Harmony (*or* Grade 3 Keyboard Harmony)
Grade 4 Harmony (*or* Grade 4 Keyboard Harmony)
Grade 4 Counterpoint
Grade 5 Harmony and Counterpoint (*or* Grade 5 Keyboard Harmony)
Grade 5 Analysis

Candidates will be considered for the Gold Medal for Excellence in Theory in the academic year in which they are eligible to graduate with an ARCT diploma. Candidates must obtain an overall average of at least 80 percent for the eight examinations.

Section 2 – Examination Requirements

EXAMINATION REPERTOIRE

The *Violin Syllabus* lists the repertoire for violin examinations. Information given for each item includes:

- ✔ the composer
- ✔ the larger work of which the selection is a part (where applicable)
- ✔ the title of the selection
- ✔ an anthology or collection in which the selection can be found (where applicable)
- ✔ performance directions (where applicable) indicating the section(s) or movement(s) of a work to be prepared
- ✔ the publisher of a suggested edition (where applicable)

Names of publishers are indicated by an assigned abbreviation. Please see p. 17 for a list of publishers with their abbreviations.

Da Capo Signs and Repeats

- When performing repertoire at an examination, candidates should observe *da capo* signs.
- Repeat signs should ordinarily be ignored.

Memory

- In Grades 1 to 6, six marks are awarded for memorization of repertoire. Full marks will be given for each repertoire selection that is completely memorized.
- In Grades 5 to 10 and ARCT, repertoire from List B (sonatas) need not be memorized.
- Candidates for Grades 7 to 10 and ARCT examinations are expected to perform repertoire from Lists A, C, and D from memory. Up to *two* marks per repertoire selection will be deducted if music is used.
- Studies/etudes and orchestral excerpts need not be memorized and no extra marks will be awarded for memory.
- Technical tests (scales, arpeggios, and double stops) *must* be played from memory.

Syllabus Repertoire Lists

The repertoire for each grade is divided into several lists, according to genre or style. Candidates are encouraged to choose a program that includes a variety of musical styles, periods, and keys.

- In the Introductory Grade and Grades 1 and 2, there are two lists:
  List A includes works in a slower tempo
  List B includes works in a faster tempo
- The repertoire for Grades 3 to 7 is divided into three lists according to genre or stylistic period. (An explanation of the lists is given at the beginning of the repertoire for each grade.)
- In Grades 8 to 10 and ARCT, there are four lists:
  List A consists of concertos
  List B consists of sonatas
  List C consists of concert pieces
  List D consists of unaccompanied works

Editions

For many repertoire items, the *Violin Syllabus* listing includes a suggested edition (indicated by an assigned publisher abbreviation). These editions have been chosen for their quality or for their availability in North America. Where no publisher is indicated, students are encouraged to use the best edition available—the edition that most accurately reflects the composer's intentions.

Fingering, bowing, and other editorial markings vary from edition to edition. Examination marks will not be deducted for altering these editorial suggestions as long as the resulting change is musically acceptable.

Availability

RCM Examinations has made every effort to ensure that most of the materials listed are in print and easily available at leading music retailers throughout North America. If you experience difficulty in obtaining violin music in your community, consult the Sources of Violin Music section on p. 78 or contact:

Royal Conservatory Music and Book Stores
273 Bloor Street West
Toronto, ON M5W 1W2
telephone: 1-866-585-2225
fax: 416-585-7801

However, please note that the publishing industry changes rapidly. Works go out of print, and copyrights move from one firm to another. In addition, the repertoire lists contain a few works that are no longer in print but that teachers or candidates may have in their personal collections. Out-of-print items are indicated in the lists as "[OP]." Candidates may use an out-of-print work for examination purposes provided they can obtain the published work. (Please see "Copyright and Photocopying" below.)

Anthologies and Collections

If a repertoire selection is published in a collection of a composer's music or in an anthology containing music by a number of composers, the title of the collection or anthology is usually included in the *Violin Syllabus* listing. Individual selections may also be found in other sources.

- In order to save space, the titles of some anthologies have been shortened. For example, *The Encore Series for Violin and Piano* appears in syllabus listings as *Encore*.
- The words "vol." and "book" have been omitted from the shortened titles. The number following the title (for example, *Encore*, 2) indicates the volume, book, or set number in which the selection can be found.
- The list of anthologies, collections, and studies in the "Bibliography" (see p. 75) provides full bibliographic information for most of the publications identified in the repertoire lists.

Violin Series, Third Edition

In order to ensure the ready availability of high-quality examination materials, The Frederick Harris Music Co., Limited has published *Violin Series, Third Edition*. This series includes nine *Repertoire Albums* (Introductory Grade through Grade 8), two books of *Violin Technique* (Introductory to Grade 4 and Grades 5 to 8), and one book of *Orchestral Excerpts* (Grades 7 to 10 and ARCT).

The *Violin Syllabus* lists a varied selection of studies for each grade. For the convenience of students and teachers, *Violin Series, Third Edition: Violin Technique* books include a number of the studies/etudes listed for each grade. These books also include all the scales and arpeggios required for examinations.

Orchestral Excerpts

All orchestral excerpts listed in the *Violin Syllabus* are included in *Violin Series, Third Edition: Orchestral Excerpts*. Candidates may select the specified passages from standard violin orchestral parts.

Copyright and Photocopying

Composers, artists, editors, and publishers rely on sales revenues to contribute to their livelihood. Photocopying music deprives the creators of due compensation.

Please note that photocopied music will not be permitted in the examination room. Candidates who bring photocopies to the examination will not be examined.

Candidates should bring all music to be performed to the examination. Candidates who wish to photocopy one page of a selection for the purpose of facilitating a page turn may do so with permission from the publisher. The Frederick Harris Music Co., Limited is pleased to grant permission to festival, recital, and examination participants to photocopy one page from Frederick Harris Music publications for the purpose of facilitating a page turn.

REPERTOIRE SUBSTITUTIONS

Candidates in Grades 1 to 10 and ARCT who wish to expand their choice of examination repertoire may replace *one* selection from the repertoire listed for their grade with a substitute selection.

For candidates in Grades 1 to 10, the substitute selection may come from one of two sources:

- the repertoire list of the next higher grade in the *Syllabus*
- other selections not listed in the *Syllabus*.

For ARCT candidates, the substitute selection must come from other selections not listed in the *Syllabus*.

Please note that the substitute selection must replace a repertoire selection. Substitutions for studies/etudes and orchestral excerpts are not permitted.

There are three types of substitute selections:

Syllabus Substitutions
Non-*Syllabus* Substitutions
Own Choice Substitutions

	Permitted in	Description of Substitute Selection	Prior Approval Required
***Syllabus* Substitutions**	Grades 1–10	Must be chosen from the corresponding list of the next higher grade in the *Syllabus*	No
Non-*Syllabus* Substitutions	Grades 1–10, ARCT	Must be of equal difficulty and musical quality to works listed in the *Syllabus* for that grade	Yes
Own Choice Substitutions	Grades 9, 10, ARCT	Replaces a selection from List D only. Must be of equal difficulty and musical quality to works listed in the *Syllabus* for that grade	No

Syllabus Substitutions

- Prior approval is not required.
- Replacement selections must be chosen from the corresponding list of the next higher grade in the *Syllabus*. (For example, a candidate for Grade 7 might choose a selection from List B of Grade 8 to replace a selection from List B of Grade 7.)
- The replacement selection must be performed exactly as listed in the *Syllabus*.

Non-*Syllabus* Substitutions

- Prior approval is required.
- The replacement selection must be of equal difficulty and musical quality to works listed in the *Syllabus* for that grade.
- Candidates wishing to include a Non-*Syllabus* Substitution on their examination programs should complete a Non-*Syllabus* Substitution form (available at www.rcmexaminations.org). Send the form, together with the appropriate fee and a copy of the substitute piece, to RCM Examinations. (Photocopies used for this purpose should be marked "For Approval Only"; these photocopies will be destroyed once a decision has been made.) Published music will be returned along with the approved form.
- Non-*Syllabus* Substitution forms must be received before the application deadline.
- Bring the approved Non-*Syllabus* Substitution form to your examination and give it to the examiner.
- Candidates are advised to prepare an alternate work in case the request is denied. *Please note that marks will be deducted from the final examination mark for the use of an unapproved piece.*

Own Choice Substitutions

- Prior approval is not required.
- Replacement selections for Own Choice Substitutions may be used only to replace a repertoire selection from List D.
- The replacement selection must be of equal difficulty and musical quality to works listed in the *Syllabus* for that grade.
- Judgment shown in choosing a substitute selection will be considered in the marking. For this reason, RCM Examinations will not answer questions or give advice regarding Own Choice Substitutions. It is the responsibility of the teacher to provide the appropriate advice.
- Candidates should clearly indicate such replacement selections as "Own Choice" on the list of repertoire to be handed to the examiner.

EXAMINATION PROCEDURES

Candidates must be ready to perform at least fifteen minutes before their scheduled time. *Please note that candidate examination times cannot be exchanged.*

- The availability of tune-up rooms cannot be guaranteed.
- The availability of music stands cannot be guaranteed.
- The candidate's performance may be interrupted at the examiner's discretion when an assessment has been reached.
- Examiners are not permitted to assist candidates in tuning their instruments. A teacher or assistant should be on hand to assist candidates who cannot tune accurately.
- Page-turners and other assistants are not permitted in the examination room. Waiting areas are provided for parents, teachers, and assistants.

Music

- Candidates should list all repertoire to be performed on their examination schedule and bring it to the examination.
- Candidates should bring all music to be performed to the examination, whether or not selections are memorized. For works requiring accompaniment, bring two copies: one for the examiner and one for the accompanist. *Please note that photocopied music is not permitted in the examination room unless the candidate has a letter of permission from the publisher.* (Please see "Copyright and Photocopying" on p. 13.)

Accompanists

- Candidates must provide their own accompanists. Taped accompaniments are not permitted. *Candidates who do not provide an accompanist will not be examined.*
- All selections requiring accompaniment must be performed with piano accompaniment only. No other instruments are permitted.
- Accompanists are permitted in the examination room only while they are playing accompaniments for the candidate.

Candidates with Special Needs

- Candidates with special needs are asked to apply in writing to RCM Examinations prior to the examination application deadline and give details concerning their needs. Each case will be dealt with individually.
- Candidates with special needs may receive assistance in and out of the examination room, but helpers must remain in the waiting area during the actual examination.

TABLE OF MARKS

	Grades 1–2	Grades 3–4	Grade 5	Grade 6	Grade 7	Grades 8–9	Grade 10	Teacher's ARCT	Performer's ARCT
Repertoire	54	54	54	54	50	50	50 (35)	20 (14)	80
List A	27	18	17	17	15	15	16		20
List B	27	18	20	20	20	15	14	*(no mark*	20
List C	–	18	17	17	15	10	10	*breakdown)*	20
List D	–	–	–	–	–	10	10		20
Memory	6	6	6	6	–	–	–	–	–
Orchestral Excerpts	–	–	–	–	10	10	10 (7)	10 (7)	20
Technical Requirements	30	20	20	20	20	20	20 (14)	10 (7)	–
Studies/Etudes	15	10	10	10	10	10	10	–	–
Technical Tests	15	10	10	10	10	10	10	10	–
Ear Tests	10	10	10	10	10	10	10 (7)	10 (7)	–
Metre	–	–	–	–	–	–	–	2	–
Rhythm	5	3	3	2	2	–	–	–	–
Intervals	–	3	3	3	3	3	2	2	–
Chords	–	–	–	2	2	2	2	3	–
Cadences	–	–	–	–	–	2	3	–	–
Playback	5	4	4	3	3	3	3	3	–
Sight Reading	–	10	10	10	10	10	10 (7)	10 (7)	–
Sight Reading	–	7	7	7	7	7	7	4 + 4	–
Sight Clapping	–	3	3	3	3	3	3	2	–
Viva Voce	–	–	–	–	–	–	–	40	–
(a) Pedagogical Principles	–	–	–	–	–	–	–	10 (7)	–
(b) Applied Pedagogy	–	–	–	–	–	–	–	30 (21)	–
TOTALS	100	100	100	100	100	100	100	100	100

- No marks are given for the Introductory examination. The examiner will prepare a written critique and all candidates will receive a certificate of accomplishment.
- In Grades 1 through 4, the mark for Technical Tests covers the performance of scales and arpeggios. In Grades 5 through ARCT, the mark for Technical Tests covers the performance of scales, arpeggios, and double stops.
- To qualify for the ARCT examination, Grade 10 candidates must achieve either an overall mark of 75 *or* a minimum of 70 percent in *each* section of the examination. (In the "Table of Marks," 70-percent figures are given in parentheses.)
- Performer's ARCT candidates must achieve an overall mark of 70 in order to pass.
- Teacher's ARCT candidates must achieve either an overall mark of 75 *or* a minimum of 70 percent in *each* section of the examination in order to pass. (In the "Table of Marks," 70-percent figures are given in parentheses.)
- There is no mark breakdown for the Repertoire section of the Teacher's ARCT examination.

CLASSIFICATION OF MARKS

Grades 1 to 10

First Class Honours with Distinction	90–100
First Class Honours	80–89
Honours	70–79
Pass	60–69
Grade 10 ARCT prerequisite	75 overall *or* 70% in each section

Performer's and Teacher's ARCT

First Class Honours with Distinction	90–100
First Class Honours	80–89
Honours	70–79
Pass (Performer's)	70
Pass (Teacher's)	75 overall *or* 70% in each section

SUPPLEMENTAL EXAMINATIONS

Supplemental examinations are offered for any section, except Repertoire, of a Grade 10 or Teacher's ARCT practical examination for candidates who wish to improve their mark in a particular section of an examination, according to the following conditions:

- Supplemental examinations are not available for the Repertoire section of an examination.
- Supplemental examinations are taken during regularly scheduled examination sessions.
- A supplemental examination comprises only *one section* of an examination.
- Candidates may take a maximum of *two* supplemental examinations per complete examination.
- Any supplemental examinations must be completed within *two years* of the date of the original examination.

Grade 10
In order to be eligible to take a supplemental examination in Grade 10, candidates must have attempted the complete examination within the last two years, achieved a *minimum total mark of 65*, and obtained *at least 70 percent* in the Repertoire section of the examination.

Teacher's ARCT
In order to be eligible to take a supplemental examination at the ARCT level, candidates must achieve the minimum marks specified in the following table.

Please note that supplemental examinations are not offered for the Performer's ARCT in Violin.

Summary of Supplemental Examination Policies

	Grade 10	Teacher's ARCT
To achieve pass standing	60% in order to receive certificate once theory co-requisites are complete	70% in each section of Part 1 *and* 70% in each section of Part 2 *and* 70% in Part 3 within a *two-year* time period *or* overall mark of 75 in Parts 1 and 2 combined *and* 70% in Part 3 within a *two-year* time period
To achieve standing to proceed to ARCT	70% in each section *or* overall mark of 75%	—
Reasons for taking supplemental examination	to reach 70% standing in each section *or* to upgrade mark in one section that is already at 70%	to reach 70% standing in each section *or* to upgrade mark on one section that is already at 70%
Eligibility for taking a supplemental examination for Grade 10	overall mark of 65% *and* 70% in Repertoire section	—
Eligibility for taking a supplemental examination for Teacher's ARCT, Part 1	—	70% in Repertoire section
Eligibility for taking a supplemental examination for Teacher's ARCT, Part 2	—	70% in either *Viva Voce* A or *Viva Voce* B
Number of supplemental examinations allowed	two	one in Part 1 one in Part 2
Time limit to complete supplemental examinations	*two years* from the date of the original examination	*two years* from the date of the original examination

ABBREVIATIONS

Names of Publishers

The following abbreviations identify publishers listed throughout the *Violin Syllabus*. When no publisher or edition is indicated for a specific piece, the work is available in several standard editions. For more information, please see "Examination Repertoire" on pp. 12–13.

ABR Associated Board of the Royal Schools of Music (London)
AEN Aeneas Press (Toronto)
AUG Augener & Co. (London)
B&H Boosey & Hawkes (London, New York) *www.boosey.com*
BAR Bärenreiter *www.barenreiter.com*
BER Berandol Music
BMC Boston Music Co.
BOS Bosworth & Co. Ltd. (UK)
BRD Broude International Editions, Inc.
BRH Breitkopf & Härtel (Wiesbaden) *www.breitkopf.com*
CAN Cantus Music
CHS J & W Chester Ltd.
CMC available from Canadian Music Centre (Toronto, Calgary, Vancouver, Montreal) *www.musiccentre.ca*
CMS Children's Music Series (Ann Arbor, Michigan)
DOB Doblinger Musikverlag (Vienna) *www.doblinger.at*
DOM Les Éditions Doberman-Yppan (St. Nicolas, Quebec) *www.dobermaneditions.com*
DUR Durand et Cie (Paris)
ECK EC Kirby (Toronto)
ELK Elkin Co. Music Publishers (London)
EMB Editio Musica Budapest
EVO Elkan-Vogel Co., Inc.
FAB Faber Music Ltc. (London) *www.fabermusic.com*
FHM The Frederick Harris Music Co., Ltd. (Mississauga, Ontario) *www.frederickharrismusic.com*
FIS Carl Fischer Music (New York) *www.carlfischer.com*
FOL Charles Foley Publications (New York)
GVT Gordon V. Thompson Music (Alfred Publishing)
HAL Hal Leonard Corporation (Milwaukee, Wisconsin) *www.halleonard.com*
HEN G. Henle Verlag (Munich)
HMP Haydn-Mozart Presse (Salzburg)
INT International Music Co.
KAL Edwin F. Kalmus (Opa Locka, Florida) *www.kalmus-music.com*
KJO Neil A. Kjos Music Co. (San Diego, California) *www.kjos.com*
KUN Edition Kunzelman
LEE Leeds Music (Canada)
MAS Masters Music Publications (Boca Raton, Florida)
MAY Kevin Mayhew Publishers (Suffolk) *www.kevinmayhewltd.com*
MCA MCA Canada Ltd.
NAG Nagels Music Verlag
NOV Novello & Co. Ltd.
NWW New World
OME Omega Music Company
OTT Schott Music International *www.schott-music.com*
OUP Oxford University Press (London, New York)
PER Peer International
PET Edition Peters
PRE Theodore Presser Company (Bryn Mawr, Pennsylvania)
PWM Polskie Wydawnictwo Muzyczne (Krakow)
RCM available from Royal Conservatory Music and Book Store
RIC G. Ricordi & Co. (Milan) *www.ricordi.com*
S&B Stainer & Bell
SCH G. Schirmer Inc. (New York)
SIM N. Simrock Publishers (London-Hamburg)
SUM Summy-Birchard Inc. (Alfred Publishing)
UMU United Music Publishers
UNI Universal Edition Inc. (Vienna, London, New York)
WAR Warner Bros. Publications (Alfred Publishing)
WAT Waterloo Music Publications (Waterloo, Ontario) *www.waterloomusic.com*

Other Abbreviations and Symbols

arr. arranged by
attr. attributed to
bk book
ed. edited by
m., mm. measure(s)
mvt movement
no. number
[OP] out of print
op. opus
p., pp. page(s)
rev. revised
trans. translated by
transc. transcribed by
vol. volume

• represents one selection for examination purposes
→ parts or sections of works to be performed at examinations

THEMATIC CATALOGUES

Opus numbers and Catalogue Numbers

"Opus" (op.) is a term used with a number to designate the position of a given work in the chronological sequence of works by the composer. However, these numbers are often an unreliable guide, and may have been assigned by a publisher rather than the composer. Sometimes a single work will have conflicting opus numbers. Certain genres, such as operas and other vocal works, were not always assigned opus numbers. For these reasons, individual works by a number of composers are identified by numbers assigned in scholarly thematic catalogues. Some of the more important thematic catalogues are listed below.

Anhang

Some catalogue numbers include the prefix "Anh." (for example, BWV Anh.121). "Anh." is an abbreviation for *Anhang,* a German word meaning appendix or supplement.

WoO

Some catalogue numbers include the prefix "WoO" (for example, WoO 63). "WoO" is an abbreviation for *Werk ohne Opuszahl* (work without opus number). These numbers are used to designate works for which the composer did not assign an opus number.

Johann Sebastian Bach

Works by J.S. Bach are identified by "BWV" numbers (for example, Allemande in G Minor, BWV 836). "BWV" is the abbreviation for *Bach-Werke-Verzeichnis*, the short title of the *Thematisch-systematisches Verzeichnis der musikalischen Werke von Johann Sebastian Bach* (Leipzig, 1950), a thematic catalogue of Bach's complete works originally compiled by the German music librarian Wolfgang Schmieder.

George Frideric Handel

Works by George Frideric Handel are identified by "HWV" numbers (for example, Gavotte in G Major, HWV 491). "HWV" is an abbreviation for *Handel Werke Verzeichnis.* The full title for this thematic catalogue, compiled by Margaret and Walter Eisen, is *Händel-Handbuch, gleichzeitig Suppl. zu Hallische Händel-Ausgabe* (Kassel: Bärenreiter, 1978–1986).

Franz Joseph Haydn

Works by Haydn are identified by Hoboken numbers (for example, Sonata in D Major, Hob. XVI:37). Anthony van Hoboken was a Dutch musicologist. His thematic catalogue, *Joseph Haydn: Thematisch-bibliographisches Werkverzeichnis* (Mainz, B. Schott, 1957–1971) divides Haydn's works into a number of categories that are indicated by Roman numerals.

Wolfgang Amadeus Mozart

Works by Mozart are identified by "K" numbers (for example, Sonata in C Major, K 545). "K" stands for *Köchel Verzeichnis* first published in 1862. Ludwig Ritter von Köchel (1800–1877) was an Austrian professor of botany who devoted his retirement years to collecting all the known works by Mozart. He created a chronological catalogue in which these works are listed and numbered.

Henry Purcell

Works by Henry Purcell are identified by Z numbers (for example, Minuet in G major, Z 651). These numbers were assigned by Franklin B. Zimmerman in his thematic catalogue of Purcell's works, *Henry Purcell: An Analytical Catalogue of his Music* (London: MacMillan, 1963).

Franz Schubert

Works by Franz Schubert are identified by "Deutsch" numbers (for example, Waltz in A flat, op. 9, no. 12, D 365). These numbers were assigned by Otto Erich Deutsch (1883–1967) in his thematic catalogue of Schubert's works, *Thematisches Verzeichnis seiner Werke in chronologischer Folge (Neue Schubert Ausgabe* Serie VIII, Bd. 4, Kassell, 1978).

Georg Philipp Telemann

Works by Georg Philipp Telemann are identified by "TWV" numbers (for example, Fantasia in D Minor, TWV 33:2). "TWV" is an abbreviation for *Telemann Werkverzeichnis.* This thematic catalogue—*Thematischer-Systematisches Verzeichnis seiner Werke: Telemann Werkverzeichnis* (Kassel: Bärenreiter, 1984)—was compiled by Martin Runke.

Antonio Vivaldi

Works by Antonio Vivaldi are identified by "RV" numbers and/or by "F" numbers. "RV" is an abbreviation for *Ryom Verzeichnis.* This thematic catalogue of Vivaldi's works—*Verzeichnis der Werke Antonio Vivaldis (RV): kleine Ausgabe* (Leipzig: Deutscher Verlag für Musik, 1974, 2nd ed. 1979) was compiled by Peter Ryom. The F numbers were assigned by Antonio Fanna in *Opere strumentali di Antonio Vivaldi (1678–1741): catalogo numerico-tematico secondo la catalogazione Fanna* (Milan, 1986).

Section 3 – Practical Examinations

TECHNICAL REQUIREMENTS

Studies/Etudes

A selection of studies/etudes for the Introductory Grade examination and Grades 1 through 8 is published in *Violin Series, Third Edition: Violin Technique Introductory–4* and *Violin Technique 5–8* (Mississauga, Ontario: Frederick Harris Music, 2006). In all grades, studies/etudes need not be memorized and no extra marks will be awarded for memory. For complete details on examination requirements for studies/etudes, please consult the listings for each grade.

Technical Tests

For complete information regarding technical tests, please refer to the charts for each grade. Complete technical tests are published in *Violin Series, Third Edition: Violin Technique Introductory–4* and *Violin Technique 5–8* (Mississauga, Ontario: Frederick Harris Music, 2006).

General Instructions

- All scales, arpeggios, and broken and solid double stops are to be played from memory, ascending and descending, in the stated keys, with the required bowings. Candidates may use either the suggested fingering or another logical pattern.
- Metronome markings given in the chart for each grade indicate minimum speed.
- Intonation, tone quality, and fluency are important factors in the evaluation of a candidate's performance.

Three-Octave Scales

Please note that candidates must use the correct three-octave scale patterns for their grade.

- Candidates for Grade 6 must use the following three-octave pattern.

- Candidates for Grades 7, 8, 9, 10, and Teacher's ARCT must use the Galamian pattern.

Introductory Grade

The Introductory Violin Examination is intended to give beginning violin students the experience of playing for an examiner in a non-competitive, friendly atmosphere. No marks are given, but the examiner will prepare an encouraging, positive written critique. All candidates will receive a certificate of accomplishment.

REPERTOIRE

Please see "Examination Repertoire" on pp. 12–13 for important information regarding this section of the examination.

Candidates should be prepared to play *two* contrasting selections: one from List A and one from List B.

- List A includes pieces in a slower tempo.
- List B includes pieces in a faster tempo.

Each bulleted item (•) represents one selection for examination purposes. Compositions marked with an asterisk (*) are included in *Violin Series, Third Edition: Introductory* (Mississauga, Ontario: Frederick Harris Music, 2006).

LIST A

Bayly, Thomas H.
• **Long, Long Ago** (in *Suzuki Violin School,* 1 SUM)

Bennett, Richard Rodney
• **Serenade** (in *Up Bow, Down Bow* NOV)

Blachford, Frank
Three Rhythmical Pieces
* • **Berceuse** FHM

Colledge, Katherine, and Hugh Colledge
Wagon Wheels B&H
• **Full Moon**

Coulthard, Jean
• **A Quiet Moment** (in *Encore,* 1 FHM)

de Keyser, Paul
* • **Poème** (in *Violin Playtime,* 1 FAB)

Duke, David
* • **All Alone** (in *Encore,* 1 FHM)

Hayes, Philip
* • **Canon** (arr. Paul de Keyser, in *Young Violinist's Repertoire,* 1 FAB)

Huws Jones, Edward
Really Easy Violin Book FAB
* • **Dinosaur Plod**

Hyslop, Ricky
Music Stands FHM
* • **Spaceman**

Kadosa, Pál
* • **Andante cantabile** EMB

Rose, Michael
Fiddler's Ten NOV
* • **Reverie**
• **Song**

Telfer, Nancy
Leading a Dog's Life
* • **Time for a Nap**

LIST B

Traditional
• **Go Tell Aunt Rhody** (in *Suzuki Violin School,* 1 SUM)
* • **J'ai du bon tabac** (arr. Hugh J. McLean FHM)
• **May Song** (in *Suzuki Violin School,* 1 SUM)
• **O Come, Little Children** (in *Suzuki Violin School,* 1 SUM)
* • **Playing Ball** (arr. Stephen Chatman FHM)
• **Song of the Wind** (in *Suzuki Violin School,* 1 SUM)

Carse, Adam
The Fiddler's Nursery S&B
* • **Dance Steps**
* • **Minuet**

Colledge, Katherine, and Hugh Colledge
Wagon Wheels B&H
• **Bell Ringers**
• **Chinese Lanterns**
• **Knickerbocker Glory**

Ethridge, Jean
• **Morris Dance** (in *Encore,* 1 FHM)
* • **The Subway Train** (in *Encore,* 1 FHM)

Huws Jones, Edward
The Really Easy Violin Book FAB
* • **Boogie**

Kabalevsky, Dmitri
• **Peter** (in *Kabalevsky: Albumstücke* PET)
Twenty Pieces for Violin and Piano, op. 80 MCA
* • **A Stroll**

Krasev, A.
* • **Pony Trot** (in *Young Violinist's Repertoire,* 1 FAB)

Nelson, Sheila M.
Piece by Piece, 2 B&H
* • **Merry-Go-Round**

Rose, Michael
Fiddler's Ten NOV
• **March**

Susato, Tylman
* • **Ronde** (arr. FHM)

Suzuki, Shin'ichi
• **Allegro** (in *Suzuki Violin School,* 1 SUM)

TECHNICAL REQUIREMENTS

Please see "Technical Requirements" on p. 19 for important information regarding this section of the examination.

Studies/Etudes

Candidates should be prepared to play *one* selection from the following list. Compositions marked with an asterisk (*) are included in *Violin Series, Third Edition: Violin Technique Introductory–4* (Mississauga, Ontario: Frederick Harris Music, 2006). Each bulleted item (•) represents one selection for examination purposes.

Anderson, Gerald E. and Robert S. Frost
All for Strings: A Comprehensive String Method, 1 KJO
* • **D Scale Waltz**

Avsharian, Evelyn
Fun with Basics: Children's Music Series CMS
• ***one* of nos. 1, 6, 7**

de Keyser, Paul
Violin Playtime Studies FAB
• ***one* of nos. 3, 5, *7** (Tick-Tock Quavers), **8, 11, 13**

Technical Tests

Please see "Technical Tests" on p. 19 for important information regarding this section of the examination.

Scales

Please note that all scales must be played from memory. Please refer to *Violin Series, Third Edition: Violin Technique Introductory–4* for required patterns.

Scales	Keys	Range	Tempo	Bowing
Major	D, A	1 octave	♩ = 60	♩ ♩

EAR TESTS

Rhythm

Candidates will be asked to sing, clap, or tap the rhythm of a short melody after it has been played *twice* by the examiner.

– *time signatures:* $\frac{2}{4}$ or $\frac{3}{4}$

Melody Playback

Candidates will be asked to play back a four-note melody, either on the violin or on the piano. The melody will be based on the first three notes of the major scale. The examiner will name the key, play the tonic triad *once*, and play the melody *twice*.

– *beginning note:* tonic (open string)
– *keys:* D or A major

SIGHT READING

Sight reading is not required in the Introductory Grade.

THEORY CO-REQUISITES

None

Grade 1

REPERTOIRE

Please see "Examination Repertoire" on pp. 12–13 for important information regarding this section of the examination.

Candidates should be prepared to play *two* contrasting selections: one from List A and one from List B.

- List A includes pieces in a slower tempo.
- List B includes pieces in a faster tempo.

Each bulleted item (•) represents one selection for examination purposes. Compositions marked with an asterisk (*) are included in *Violin Series, Third Edition: Repertoire 1* (Mississauga, Ontario: Frederick Harris Music, 2006).

LIST A

Traditional
* • **All Through the Night** (arr. Barbara Barber, in *Solos for Young Violinists* SUM)
* • **Evening Song** (*Der lieben Sonnen, Licht und Pracht*, BWV 466, arr. FHM)

Archer, Violet
Twelve Miniatures WAT
* • **On Tiptoe**

Carse, Adam
Fiddle Fancies S&B
* • **Bluebell Chimes**

Coulthard, Jean
* • **The Sailboat on the Lake** (in *Encore,* 1 FHM)

Elgar, Edward
Six Easy Pieces, op. 22 FAB; BOS
• **no. 1**
• **no. 3**
• **no. 4**

Handel, George Frideric
* • **Air from *Rinaldo***, (arr. Eric Thiman ABR)

Hyslop, Ricky
Music Stands FHM
* • **Roumanian Dance**
• **T.V. Theme**

Kabalevsky, Dmitri
• **Traurige Erzählung**, op. 39, no. 16 (in *Kabalevsky: Albumstücke* PET)
• **Unser Land** (in *Kabalevsky: Albumstücke* PET)
Twenty Pieces for Violin and Piano, op. 80 MCA
• **A Song**

Lawes, Henry
* • **A Canzonet** (arr. Thomas Dunhill ABR)

Mozart, Wolfgang Amadeus
• **Lied** (in *Young Violinist's Repertoire,* 2 FAB)

Rose, Michael
Fiddler's Ten NOV
• **On the Swing**

Schumann, Robert
* • **Cradle Song**, op. 124, no. 6 (arr. FHM)

Sugár, Rezső
* • **Song and Dance** (in *Violin Music for Beginners* EMB)
→ complete

Suzuki, Shin'ichi
• **Andantino** (in *Suzuki Violin School,* 1 SUM)

LIST B

Anonymous
• **Contredanse** (in *Violin Playtime,* 2 FAB)

Archer, Violet
Twelve Miniatures WAT
• **Jig**

Bach, Johann Sebastian
• **Minuet 1**, (arr. from Suite in G Minor, BWV 822 in *Suzuki Violin School,* 1 SUM)

Carse, Adam
The Fiddler's Nursery S&B
• **A Bumpkin's Dance**
• **At Dawn**

Colledge, Katherine, and Hugh Colledge
Fast Forward B&H
• **Singapore Sunset**

Elgar, Edward
Six Easy Pieces, op. 22 FAB; BOS
• **no. 2**
• **no. 5**
• **no. 6**

Ethridge, Jean
* • **Homage to Bartók** (in *Encore,* 1 FHM)

Fleming, Robert
* • **Scotty Lad** FHM

Gardner, Samuel
Journey through the Forest BMC
* • **Cuckoo Serenade**

Handel, George Frideric
• **Chorus**, from *Judas Maccabaeus* (in *Suzuki Violin School,* 2 SUM)
* • **March**, from *Scipione* (arr. Paul Jenkins FHM)

Hyslop, Ricky
Music Stands FHM
• **Autumn Parade**
• **Rapido**

Kabalevsky, Dmitri
Twenty Pieces for Violin and Piano, op. 80 MCA
• **Games**
• **March**

Mackay, Neil
Four Modern Dance Pieces S&B
• **Cha-Cha**

Murray, Eleanor
* • **The Gypsy Fiddler** (in *Tunes for My Violin* B&H)

Nelson, Sheila M.
Piece by Piece, 1 B&H
• **Flag Dance**
* • **Whirlpool Waltz**

Norton, Christopher
Microjazz for Starters B&H
* • **Snooker Table**

Pracht, Robert
• **Scherzo** (in *Twelve Easy Pieces,* op. 12 BMC)

Prelleur, Peter
• **March in A** (in *Piece by Piece,* 2 B&H)

Rose, Michael
Fiddler's Ten NOV
• **Pony Ride**

Suzuki, Shin'ichi
• **Allegretto** (in *Suzuki Violin School,* 1 SUM)

TECHNICAL REQUIREMENTS

Please see "Technical Requirements" on p. 19 for important information regarding this section of the examination.

Studies/Etudes

Candidates should be prepared to play *two* contrasting selections by different composers from the following list. Compositions marked with an asterisk (*) are included in *Violin Series, Third Edition: Violin Technique Introductory–4* (Mississauga, Ontario: Frederick Harris Music, 2006). Each bulleted item (•) represents one selection for examination purposes.

Anonymous
• **Bow Control**
* • **Finger Action**
• **Tone Control**

Cohen, Mary
Superstudies, 1 FAB
* • **Space Walk**

de Keyser, Paul
Violin Playtime Studies FAB
• ***one* of nos.** *8 (Puppet on Two Strings), **14**, **17**, **25**

Kinsey, Herbert
Elementary and Progressive Studies ABR
• ***one* of nos. 1, 2, 5, 7**

Romberg, Bernhard Heinrich
* • **Andante** (arr. A. Baird Knechtel, in *27 Etudes for Strings* GVT)

Suzuki, Shin'ichi
• **Étude** (in *Suzuki Violin School,* 1 SUM)
→ with variation
• **Perpetual Motion** (in *Suzuki Violin School,* 1 SUM)
→ with variation

Technical Tests

Please see "Technical Tests" on p. 19 for important information regarding this section of the examination.

Scales and Arpeggios

Please note that all scales and arpeggios must be played from memory. Please refer to *Violin Series, Third Edition: Violin Technique Introductory–4* for required patterns.

Scales	Keys	Range	Tempo	Bowing
Major	G, A	2 octaves	♩ = 69	♩ ♩
Melodic minor	G, A	1 octave *start on open string*		
Arpeggios				
Major	G, A	2 octaves	♩ = 69	♩ ♩ ♩
Minor	G, A	1 octave *start on open string*		

EAR TESTS

Rhythm

Candidates will be asked to sing, clap, or tap the rhythm of a short melody after it has been played *twice* by the examiner.

– *time signatures:* $\frac{2}{4}$ or $\frac{3}{4}$

Melody Playback

Candidates will be asked to play back a four-note melody, either on the violin or on the piano. The melody will be based on the first three notes of the major scale and may contain repeated notes and a leap of a 3rd. The examiner will name the key, play the tonic triad *once*, and play the melody *twice*.

– *beginning note*: tonic
– *keys*: D or A major

SIGHT READING

Sight reading is not required in Grade 1.

THEORY CO-REQUISITES

None

Grade 2

REPERTOIRE

Please see "Examination Repertoire" on pp. 12–13 for important information regarding this section of the examination.

Candidates should be prepared to play *two* contrasting selections: one from List A and one from List B.

- List A includes pieces in a slower tempo.
- List B includes pieces in a faster tempo.

Each bulleted item (•) represents one selection for examination purposes. Compositions marked with an asterisk (*) are included in *Violin Series, Third Edition: Repertoire 2* (Mississauga, Ontario: Frederick Harris Music, 2006).

LIST A

Anonymous
• **Passamezzo antico** (in *Young Violinist's Repertoire,* 3 FAB)

Archer, Violet
Twelve Miniatures WAT
* • **In Church**

Bach, Johann Sebastian
• **Musette** (arr. from English Suite no. 3, BWV 808 in *Suzuki Violin School,* 2 SUM)

Barnes, Milton
• **Three Folk Dances** CMC
→ no. 2

Bennett, Richard Rodney
* • **A Little Elegy** (in *Up Bow, Down Bow*) NOV

Coulthard, Jean
* • **A Little Sorrow** (in *Encore,* 2 FHM)

Ethridge, Jean
• **Cradle Song** (in *Encore,* 2 FHM)

Fesca, Alexander
• **Abendlied** (in *Young Violinist's Repertoire,* 1 FAB)

Halvorsen, Johan
* • **Mélodie** (arr. Warren Mould FHM)

Heins, Donald
* • **The Bell Boy Suite** FHM
→ Prelude *OR* Aria *and* Bourrée

Hook, James
• **Tempo di menuetto** (arr. Alfred Moffat, in *Old Masters for Young Players* OTT)

Hyslop, Ricky
Music Stands FHM
• **Violin Valentine**

Kabalevsky, Dmitri
Twenty Pieces for Violin and Piano, op. 80 MCA
• **Melody**

McDougall, Barbara
* • **Tall Ships** (arr. Judith McIvor FHM)

Murray, Eleanor, and Phyllis Tate
Tunes for My Violin B&H
• **Song of the Roads**
* • **The Swan**

Negely, I.
• **Pastorale** (in *Young Violinist's Repertoire,* 2 FAB)

Pracht, Robert
* • **Romance** (from *Twelve Easy Pieces,* op. 12 BMC)

Rameau, Jean-Philippe
* • **Two Sarabandes**, from *Premier livre de pièces de clavecin* (arr. Alfred Moffat, in *Old Fiddle Pieces* OTT)

Rose, Michael
Fiddler's Ten NOV
• **The Old Castle**
• **Sad Story**

LIST B

Anonymous
• **Untitled Reel 1** (arr. John Beckwith, in *Eight Miniatures from the Allen Ash Manuscript* FHM)

Traditional
* • **Vive la canadienne!** (arr. Hugh McLean FHM)

Archer, Violet
Twelve Miniatures WAT
• **Waltzing**

Babell, William
• **Two Matelottes** (arr. Alfred Moffat, in *Old Masters for Young Players* OTT)

Bach, Carl Philipp Emanuel
* • **Marche**, BWV Anh. 122 (arr. Constance Seely-Brown FIS)

Bach, Johann Sebastian
• **Minuet 2** (anon.: arr. from the Anna Magdalena Bach Notebook BWV 116; attr. to J.S. Bach, in *Suzuki Violin School,* 1 SUM)
• **Minuet 3** (Christian Petzold: arr. from the Anna Magdalena Bach Notebook BWV 114; attr. to J.S. Bach, in *Suzuki Violin School,* 1 SUM)

Bayly, Thomas H.
- **Long, Long Ago** (in *Suzuki Violin School,* 2 SUM)
  → with variation

Boismortier, Joseph Bodin de
- **Allemande** (in *Young Violinist's Repertoire,* 2 FAB)

Colledge, Katherine, and Hugh Colledge
Shooting Stars B&H
- **Cakewalk**
- **Coconuts and Mangoes**
- **Five a Side**
- **Look Lively**

Coutts, George
* • **A Pirate Bold** WAR

Duke, David
- **Motorcycles** (in *Encore,* 2 FHM)

Ethridge, Jean
* • **"Wrong Note" Caprice** (in *Encore,* 2 FHM)

Fleming, Robert
* • **Singer Man** FHM

Grechaninov, Alexandr T.
- **The Jester** OTT

Handel, George Frideric
- **Bourrée** (arr. from Sonata in F Major for oboe and basso continuo, HWV 363, in *Suzuki Violin School,* 2 SUM)

Haydn, Franz Joseph
* • **Menuet alla Zingarese** (arr. Stephen Chatman from String Quartet in D Major, op. 20, no.4 Hob. III:34 FHM)
- **Minuet and Trio** (arr. Sheila M. Nelson from Baryton Trio in D Major, Hob. XI:34, in *Piece by Piece,* 1 B&H)

Kabalevsky, Dmitri
Twenty Pieces for Violin and Piano, op. 80 MCA
- **Dance Song**
* • **Polka**
- **Skipping and Hopping**

Nelson, Sheila M.
Moving Up B&H
* • **Roger's Reel**

Pracht, Robert
* • **Hongrois** (from *Twelve Easy Pieces,* op. 12 BMC)

Rose, Michael
Fiddler's Ten NOV
- **Hide and Seek**

Shostakovich, Dmitri
- **Kleiner Marsch** (arr. Konstantin Fortunatow, in *Shostakovich: Albumstücke* PET)

Steibelt, Daniel
- **Divertimento** (in *Young Violinist's Repertoire,* 2 FAB)

Weber, Carl Maria von
- **Gypsy Dance** (in *Young Violinist's Repertoire,* 3 FAB)
- **Hunters' Chorus**, from *Der Freischütz* (in *Suzuki Violin School,* 2 SUM)

TECHNICAL REQUIREMENTS

Please see "Technical Requirements" on p. 19 for important information regarding this section of the examination.

Studies/Etudes

Candidates should be prepared to play *two* contrasting selections by different composers from the following list. Compositions marked with an asterisk (*) are included in *Violin Series, Third Edition: Violin Technique Introductory–4* (Mississauga, Ontario: Frederick Harris Music, 2006). Each bulleted item (•) represents one selection for examination purposes.

Alard, Jean-Delphin
* • **The Swinger** (arr. A. Baird Knechtel, in *27 Etudes for Strings* GVT)

de Keyser, Paul
Violin Playtime Studies FAB
- ***one* of nos. 26, 27, 29**

Kinsey, Herbert
Elementary and Progressive Studies ABR
- ***one* of nos. 9–16**

Rapoport, Katharine
* • **Kites** FHM
  → in second position

Romberg, Bernhard Heinrich
* • **Sailing** (arr. A. Baird Knechtel, in *27 Etudes for Strings* GVT)

Sitt, Hans
Studies for the Violin, op. 32, 1 FIS
- **no. 2**
- **no. 5**

Suzuki, Shin'ichi
Position Études SUM
- **Perpetual Motion**
  → in second position; choose C major or F major

Wohlfahrt, Franz
60 Studies, op. 45, 1 SCH
- ***one* of nos. 1, 2, *8, 9**

Technical Tests

Please see "Technical Tests" on p. 19 for important information regarding this section of the examination.

Scales and Arpeggios

Please note that all scales and arpeggios must be played from memory. Please refer to *Violin Series, Third Edition: Violin Technique Introductory–4* for required patterns.

Scales	Keys	Range	Tempo	Bowing
Major	G, A, B♭	2 octaves	♪ = 80	♫‿
Melodic minor	G, A			
Harmonic minor	G, A	1 octave *start on open string*	♩ = 88	♩♩‿
Major	F	1 octave *in 2nd position*	♩ = 100	𝅗𝅥
Arpeggios				
Major Minor	G, A, B♭ G, A	2 octaves	♩ = 80	♩♩♩‿
Major	F	1 octave *in 2nd position*	♩ = 100	𝅗𝅥

EAR TESTS

Rhythm

Candidates will be asked to sing, clap, or tap the rhythm of a short melody after it has been played *twice* by the examiner.

– *time signatures:* $\frac{2}{4}$ or $\frac{3}{4}$

Intervals

Candidates may choose to:

(a) sing or hum any of the following intervals after the examiner has played the first note *once*, OR
(b) identify any of the following intervals after the examiner has played the interval *once* in broken form.
– *above a given note*: major 3rd, perfect 5th

Melody Playback

Candidates will be asked to play back a melody of approximately five notes, either on the violin or on the piano. The melody will be based on the first five notes of a major scale and may contain one or more leaps of a 3rd. The examiner will name the key, play the tonic triad *once*, and play the melody *twice*.

- *beginning notes*: tonic or dominant
- *keys*: D or A major

SIGHT READING

Sight reading is not required in Grade 2.

THEORY CO-REQUISITES

None

Grade 3

REPERTOIRE

Please see "Examination Repertoire" on pp. 12–13 for important information regarding this section of the examination.

Candidates should be prepared to play *three* contrasting selections: one from List A, one from List B, and one from List C.

- List A includes music composed during the Baroque and Classical periods.
- List B includes music composed during the Romantic period and traditional pieces.
- List C includes music composed after *ca* 1930.

Each bulleted item (•) represents one selection for examination purposes. Compositions marked with an asterisk (*) are included in *Violin Series, Third Edition: Repertoire 3* (Mississauga, Ontario: Frederick Harris Music, 2006).

LIST A

Albrechtsberger, Johann G.
* • **Minuetto in D major**, from Symphony No. 3 in D major (arr. Paul Jenkins FHM)

Arne, Thomas A.
• **Melodie in G major** (arr. Alfred Moffat, in *Old Masters for Young Players,* 1 OTT)

Bach, Johann Sebastian
• **Minuet** (Christian Petzold: arr. from the Anna Magdalena Bach Notebook BWV 114; attr. to J.S. Bach, in *Suzuki Violin School,* 3 SUM)

Beethoven, Ludwig van
• **Minuet in G major** (arr. from *Sechs Menuette*, WoO 10, no. 2, in *Suzuki Violin School,* 2 SUM)

Diabelli, Anton
• **Andante cantabile**, from op. 163, no. 4 (arr. Walter Bergmann OTT)

Gluck, Christoph Willibald
* • **Gavotte in A major**, from *Don Juan* (arr. FHM)

Gossec, François-Joseph
• **Gavotte** (in *Suzuki Violin School,* 1 SUM)

Handel, George Frideric
* • **Andante larghetto**, from *Berenice* (arr. Paul Jenkins FHM)

Hasse, Johann Adolph
• **Two Dances** (in *Old Masters for Young Players,* 1 OTT)
→ Bourrée *and* Menuett

Küchler, Ferdinand
• **Concertino in G major**, op. 11 BOS
→ *1st movement

Lully, Jean-Baptiste
• **Gavotte** (in *Suzuki Violin School,* 2 SUM)

Martini, Giovanni Battista
• **Gavotte** (in *Suzuki Violin School,* 3 SUM)

Mozart, Wolfgang Amadeus
• **Pantomime**, from *Les petits riens*, K 10 (arr. Paul de Keyser and Fanny Waterman, in *Young Violinist's Repertoire,* 4 FAB)

Purcell, Henry
* • **Hornpipe**, from *The Old Bachelor*, Z 607 (arr. FHM)

Steibelt, Daniel
• **Divertimento** (arr. Alfred Moffat, in *Old Fiddle Pieces,* OTT)

LIST B

Anonymous
• **Untitled Reel 2** (arr. John Beckwith, in *Eight Miniatures from the Allen Ash Manuscript* FHM)

Traditional
* • **Jeune fillette** (arr. Jean-Baptiste Weckerlin)
• **Maytime** (arr. in *Young Violinist's Repertoire,* 3 FAB)
* • **Skye Boat Song** (arr. Hugh J. McLean)

Baklanova, Nathalia
* • **Mazurka** (in *The Young Violinist's Repertoire,* 3 FAB)

Blachford, Frank
* • **Minor Mode** FHM

Brahms, Johannes
• **Waltz** (arr. from *Walzer*, op. 39, no.15, in *Suzuki Violin School,* 2 SUM)

Colledge, Katherine, and Hugh Colledge
Shooting Stars B&H
• **Cossacks**
• **Moto perpetuo**

Paganini, Niccolò
- **Theme**, from *Witches' Dance* (arr. in *Suzuki Violin School,* 2 SUM)

Rieding, Oskar
- **Rondo**, op. 22, no. 3 BOS

Schumann, Robert
- **The Two Grenadiers**, op. 49, no. 1 (arr. in *Suzuki Violin School,* 2 SUM)

Whitaker, John
- **Darby O'Kelly** (arr. John Beckwith, in *Eight Miniatures from the Allen Ash Manuscript* FHM)

LIST C

Archer, Violet
Twelve Miniatures WAT
- **Joyous**

Blake, Howard
The Snow Man NOV
- **Music Box Dance**

Chase, Bruce
Fiddling and Fun in First Position HAL
* • **Gabby Ghost**

Coulthard, Jean
- **Friend Squirrel** (in *Encore,* 3 FHM)
- **A Sad Waltz** (in *Encore,* 3 FHM)
- **Under the Sea** (in *Encore,* 4 FHM)

Duke, David
* • **Pibroch** (in *Encore,* 2 FHM)

Fiala, George
* • **Wallaby's Lullaby**, op. 5 BER

Fleming, Robert
- **Berceuse** CMC
* • **Whistler's Tune** FHM

Kabalevsky, Dmitri
- **Fairy Story** (in *Kabalevsky: Albumstücke* PET)

Thirty Children's Pieces, op. 27 PET
* • **Sad Story** (arr. K. Sorokin, in *Kabalevsky: Albumstücke* PET)

Twenty Pieces for Violin and Piano, op. 80 MCA
- **On Holiday**

Kroll, William
* • **Donkey Doodle** SCH

Mackay, Neil
Four Modern Dance Pieces S&B
- **Rebecca**

Nelson, Sheila M.
Moving Up Again B&H
- **Eagle's Flight**

Norton, Christopher
Microjazz for Violin B&H
- **Becalmed**
- **A Dramatic Episode**
- **Fly Away**
- **Swan Song**

Persichetti, Vincent
Masques, op. 99 EVO
* • **Masque no. 1**

Severn, Edmund
- **Perpetuum mobile** FIS

Shostakovich, Dmitri
* • **The Clockwork Doll**, from *Children's Notebook,* op. 69 (arr. K. Fortunatow, in *Shostakovich: Albumstücke* PET)

TECHNICAL REQUIREMENTS

Please see "Technical Requirements" on p. 19 for important information regarding this section of the examination.

Studies/Etudes

Candidates should be prepared to play *two* contrasting selections by different composers from the following list. Compositions marked with an asterisk (*) are included in *Violin Series, Third Edition: Violin Technique Introductory–4* (Mississauga, Ontario: Frederick Harris Music, 2006). Each bulleted item (•) represents one selection for examination purposes.

Cohen, Mary
Superstudies, 2 FAB
* • **Fivepenny Waltz**

Geringas, Yaakov
Shifting: Thirty Studies for Young Violinists FHM
- ***one* of nos. 1–17** (*4: Hide and Seek)

Kayser, Heinrich Ernst
Elementary and Progressive Studies for the Violin, op. 20 SCH; FIS
- **no. 2**
  - omit articulations
- **no. 3**

Sitt, Hans
Studies for the Violin, op. 32, 1 FIS
- **no. 3** ***or*** **no. 4**

Wohlfahrt, Franz
60 Studies, op. 45, 1 SCH
- ***one*** **of nos. 4, 5, 6, 14, *17** (Grace-note Study), **20**

Technical Tests

Please see “Technical Tests” on p. 19 for important information regarding this section of the examination.

Scales and Arpeggios

Please note that all scales and arpeggios must be played from memory. Please refer to *Violin Series, Third Edition: Violin Technique Introductory–4* for required patterns.

Scales	Keys	Range	Tempo	Bowing
Major Melodic minor Harmonic minor	B, C, D	2 octaves	♪ = 100	
Major Melodic minor Harmonic minor	G	1 octave *in 3rd position*	♩ = 60	
Chromatic on	D	1 octave *start on open D string*	♩ = 66	
Arpeggios				
Major Minor	B, C, D	2 octaves	♩ = 88	

EAR TESTS

Rhythm

Candidates will be asked to sing, clap, or tap the rhythm of a short melody after it has been played *twice* by the examiner.

– *time signatures:* $\frac{2}{4}$ or $\frac{3}{4}$

Intervals

Candidates may choose to:

(a) sing or hum any of the following intervals after the examiner has played the first note *once*, OR

(b) identify any of the following intervals after the examiner has played the interval *once* in broken form.

– *above a given note*: major 3rd, perfect 5th, perfect octave

– *below a given note*: minor 3rd, perfect 5th

Melody Playback

Candidates will be asked to play back a melody of approximately five notes, either on the violin or on the piano. The melody will be based on the first five notes of a major scale and may contain leaps of a 3rd and/or a 5th. The examiner will name the key, play the tonic triad *once*, and play the melody *twice*.

– *beginning notes*: tonic or mediant

– *keys*: G, D, or A major

SIGHT READING

1. Candidates will be asked to play a simple short melody in first position, approximately equal in difficulty to repertoire of a Grade 1 level.
2. Candidates will be asked to clap or tap the rhythm of a melody in $\frac{3}{4}$ or $\frac{4}{4}$ time. A steady pace and rhythmic accentuation are expected.

THEORY CO-REQUISITES

None

Grade 4

REPERTOIRE

Please see "Examination Repertoire" on pp. 12–13 for important information regarding this section of the examination.

Candidates should be prepared to play *three* contrasting selections: one from List A, one from List B, and one from List C.

- List A includes concertos, sonatas, and fantasias.
- List B includes music composed during the Baroque period.
- List C includes concert pieces.

Each bulleted item (•) represents one selection for examination purposes. Compositions marked with an asterisk (*) are included in *Violin Series, Third Edition: Repertoire 4* (Mississauga, Ontario: Frederick Harris Music, 2006).

LIST A

Dancla, Charles
12 Fantasies, op. 86 FIS
• **Fleuve du Tage** (no. 8)
• **Rédowa de Wallerstein** (no. 3)

Küchler, Ferdinand
• **Concertino in D major**, op. 12 BOS
→ 1st *or* 3rd movement
• **Concertino in the Style of Antonio Vivaldi**, op. 15 BOS
→ *3rd movement

Millies, Hans Mollenhauer
• **Concertino in the Style of W.A. Mozart** BOS
→ *1st movement

Mollenhauer, Eduard
* • **The Infant Paganini: Fantasia** FIS

Perlman, George
• **Concertino in A** (in *Fun with Solos* CMS)
→ 3rd movement

Portnoff, Leo
Russian Fantasias BOS
• **Russian Fantasia no. 3 in A minor**

Rieding, Oskar
• **Concertino in G major**, op. 34 BOS
→ 1st movement
• **Concerto in B minor**, op. 35 BOS
→ 1st movement
• **Concerto in D major**, op. 36 BOS
→ 3rd movement

Ruegger, Charlotte
* • **Concertante** FIS

Steibelt, Daniel
• **Sonatine**, op. 33, no. 1
→ *1st movement

LIST B

Aubert, Jacques
* • **Two Minuets** (arr. OTT)

Bach, Johann Sebastian
• **Gavotte in G minor** (*Gavotte en rondeau*, arr. from Suite in G Minor for harpsichord, BWV 822, in *Suzuki Violin School,* 3 SUM)

Corelli, Arcangelo
* • **Allegro in G minor** (arr. FHM)

Handel, George Frideric
* • **Sarabande**, from Concerto in G Minor for oboe, strings, and basso continuo, HWV 287 (arr. Harold Edwin Darke ABR)

Lully, Jean-Baptiste
• **Gavotte and Musette** (arr. Alfred Moffat, in *Old Masters for Young Players,* 1 OTT)

Nicolai, Valentin
• **Minuet** (arr. Adam Carse AUG)

Purcell, Henry
* • **Two Airs**, from *Bonduca*, Z574 and *The Double Dealer*, Z592 (arr. FHM)

Rameau, Jean-Philippe
* • **Tambourin,** from *Pièces de clavecin,* (arr. FHM)

Thomas, Ambroise
• **Gavotte**, from *Mignon* (arr. in *Suzuki Violin School,* 3 SUM)

LIST C

Baklanova, Nathalia
* • **Fast Dance** (in *The Young Violinist's Repertoire,* 3 FAB)

Boccherini, Luigi
• **Minuet** (in *Suzuki Violin School,* 2 SUM)

Bouchard, Rémi
• **Suite for Violin and Piano** BMC
→ String Along

Dvořák, Antonín
• **Humoresque** (arr. from Humoresques for Piano, op. 101, no. 7, in *Suzuki Violin School,* 3 SUM)

Ethridge, Jean
* • **Two Blues** (in *Encore,* 3 FHM)

Green, W.
• **Playful Rondo** (in *Violinists' First Solo Album* FIS)

Henry, J. Harold
• **Dance de village** BOS

Hook, James
• **My Heart Is Devoted, Dear Mary, to Thee** (arr. John Beckwith, in *Eight Miniatures from the Allen Ash Manuscript* FHM)

Hyslop, Ricky
String Knots FHM
• **Canzonetta**

Kabalevsky, Dmitri
* • **Clowns**, op. 39, no. 6 (arr. Yaakov Geringas FHM)
Twenty Pieces for Violin and Piano, op. 80 MCA
• **Ping Pong**
• **Summer Song**

Mendelssohn, Ludwig
* • **Conte sérieux**, op. 62, no. 6 BOS
• **Mosquito Dance**, op. 62, no. 5 BOS

Nelson, Sheila M.
Moving Up Again B&H
* • **Caprice**
• **Moto Perpetuo**

Palaschko, Johannes
* • **March of the Pirates**, op. 65, no. 5

Rowley, Alex
• **Canzona** ELK

Schumann, Robert
* • **Knight Rupert**, arr. from *Album for the Young,* op. 68, FHM

Somervell, Arthur
• **Autumn Song** MAY

Tchaikovsky, Pyotr Il'yich
* • **Danse napolitaine**, arr. from *Swan Lake*, FHM

Thornton, Gerry
• **Bohemian Dance** RCM

TECHNICAL REQUIREMENTS

Please see "Technical Requirements" on p. 19 for important information regarding this section of the examination.

Studies/Etudes

Candidates should be prepared to play *two* contrasting selections by different composers from the following list. Compositions marked with an asterisk (*) are included in *Violin Series, Third Edition: Violin Technique Introductory–4* (Mississauga, Ontario: Frederick Harris Music, 2006). Each bulleted item (•) represents one selection for examination purposes.

Cohen, Mary
Technique Takes Off, 2 FAB
* • **The Mill Wheel**

Geringas, Yaakov
Shifting: Thirty Studies for Young Violinists FHM
• ***one* of nos. 18–30**

Kayser, Heinrich Ernst
Elementary and Progressive Studies for the Violin, op. 20 SCH; FIS
• **no. 4**

Kinsey, Herbert
Elementary Progressive Studies, 2 ABR
* • **Preparatory Exercise for Chromatic Scales**

Sitt, Hans
Studies for the Violin, op. 32, bk 1 FIS
• **no. 6 *or* no. 7**

Trott, Josephine
Melodious Double Stops, 1 SCH
• ***one* of nos. 1–9** (*5)

Wohlfahrt, Franz
60 Studies, op. 45, 2 SCH
• ***one* of nos. 31–37** (*34)
→ omit articulations

Technical Tests

Please see "Technical Tests" on p. 19 for important information regarding this section of the examination.

Scales and Arpeggios

Please note that all scales and arpeggios must be played from memory. Please refer to *Violin Series, Third Edition: Violin Technique Introductory–4* for required patterns.

Scales	Keys	Range	Tempo	Bowing
Major	A♭, D, E♭	2 octaves	♩ = 60	
Melodic minor Harmonic minor	G♯, D, E♭			
Major Melodic minor Harmonic minor	A	1 octave *in 4th position*	♩ = 84	
Major	B	1 octave *start on A string*		
Chromatic on	E	1 octave *start on D string*		
Arpeggios				
Major	A♭, D, E♭	2 octaves	♩ = 96	
Minor	G♯, D, E♭			
Major Minor	A	1 octave *in 4th position*	♩ = 84	
Dominant 7th of G major A major	*(starting on D)* *(starting on E)*	1 octave *start on D string*	♩ = 84	
Diminished 7th of B♭ minor C minor	*(starting on A)* *(starting on B)*	1 octave *start on A string*		

EAR TESTS

Rhythm

Candidates will be asked to sing, clap, or tap the rhythm of a short melody after it has been played *twice* by the examiner.

– *time signatures:* 2/4 or 6/8

Intervals

Candidates may choose to:

(a) sing or hum any of the following intervals after the examiner has played the first note *once*, OR
(b) identify any of the following intervals after the examiner has played the interval *once* in broken form.
– *above a given note*: major and minor 3rds, perfect 4th, 5th, and octave
– *below a given note*: minor 3rd, perfect 5th, and octave

Melody Playback

Candidates will be asked to play back a melody of approximately six notes, either on the violin or on the piano. The melody will be based on the first five notes of a major scale. The examiner will name the key, play the tonic triad *once*, and play the melody *twice*.

– *beginning notes*: tonic, mediant, or dominant
– *keys*: G, D, or A major

SIGHT READING

1. Candidates will be asked to play a simple short melody in first position, approximately equal in difficulty to repertoire of a Grade 2 level.
2. Candidates will be asked to clap or tap the rhythm of a melody in $\frac{3}{4}$ or $\frac{4}{4}$ time. A steady pace and rhythmic accentuation are expected.

THEORY CO-REQUISITES

None

Grade 5

REPERTOIRE

Please see "Examination Repertoire" on pp. 12–13 for important information regarding this section of the examination.

Candidates should be prepared to play *three* contrasting selections: one from List A, one from List B, and one from List C.

- List A includes concertos, *airs variés*, and fantasias.
- List B includes sonatas and suites.
- List C includes concert pieces.

Each bulleted item (•) represents one selection for examination purposes. Compositions marked with an asterisk (*) are included in *Violin Series, Third Edition: Repertoire 5* (Mississauga, Ontario: Frederick Harris Music, 2006). Please note that the selections in List B need not be memorized.

LIST A

Bacewicz, Grazyna
• **Concertino** OTT
→ *1st movement

Dancla, Charles
12 Fantasies, op. 86 FIS
• **Austrian Hymn–Don Juan**
* • **La Cenerentola**
• **Le cor des alpes–Valse du Freischütz**
• **Dernière pensée de Weber**
• **Donna del Lago–Air suisse**
• **Les noces de Figaro–Le crociato**
• **Plaisir d'amour**
• **Les Puritains**
Airs variés, op. 89 OTT; FIS
• **no. 1 on a theme by Pacini**
• **no. 2 on a theme by Rossini**

Huber, Adolf
• **Concertino in G major**, op. 6, no. 2 FIS
→ 1st movement (to end of p. 1 of violin part)
• **Concertino in G major**, op. 8, no. 4 FIS
→ 1st movement (to D major cadence, end of p. 1 of violin part)

Járdányi, Pál
• **Concertino** EMB

Rieding, Oskar
• **Air varié**, op. 23, no. 3 BOS

Seitz, Friedrich
• **Concerto no. 5 in D major**, op. 22 (in *Suzuki Violin School*, 4 SUM)
→ 1st movement
• **Concerto no. 2 in G major**, op. 13 (in *Suzuki Violin School*, 4 SUM)
→ 3rd movement

LIST B

Corelli, Arcangelo
12 Sonate, op. 5 AUG
• **Sonata no. 7 in D minor** (arr. István Homolya AUG)
→ 1st *and* 2nd movements *OR* *3rd *and* *4th movements
• **Sonata no. 8 in E minor**
→ 1st *and* 2nd movements *OR* 3rd *and* 4th movements
• **Sonata no. 9 in A major**
→ 3rd *and* 4th movements
• **Sonata no. 10 in F major**
→ 1st *and* 2nd movements *OR* 3rd *and* 4th movements
• **Sonata no. 11 in E major**
→ 1st *and* 2nd movements *OR* 3rd *and* 4th movements

Dolin, Samuel
• **2 x 3** CMC

Pepusch, Johann Christoph
Six Sonatas, op. 1 LEE; OTT
• **Sonata no. 3 in G major** (arr. Siegfried Pritsche)
→ *1st *and* *2nd movements
• **Sonata in G major** OTT
→ 1st *and* 2nd movements *OR* 3rd *and* 4th movements

Telemann, Georg Philipp
• **Sonata no. 5**, TWV 41: E1 EMB
→ 1st (*Affetuoso-Siciliano*) *and* 4th (*Allegro*) movements

Willan, Healey
• **Sonata no. 2** BOS
→ Adagio *and* Gavotte

LIST C

Adaskin, Murray
• **Quiet Song** CMC

Bach, Johann Sebastian
• **Bourrée** (arr. from Suite for cello no. 3 in C major, BWV 1009, in *Suzuki Violin School,* 3 SUM)

Blachford, Frank
* • **Mazurka** FHM

Bohm, Carl
• **Perpetuum mobile** (from *Third Suite* BMC)

Coulthard, Jean
• **On the March** BER
* • **Music on a Hebridean Folk Song** (in *Encore,* 5 FHM)

Ethridge, Jean
* • **Jig** (in *Encore,* 5 FHM)
• **Rêverie** (in *Encore,* 4 FHM)

Gluck, Christoph Willibald
* • **Musette and Air de ballet**, from *Armide* (arr. Kathleen Wood FHM)

Haydn, Franz Joseph
* • **The Oxen Minuet**, Hob. IX:27 (arr. FHM)

Heins, Donald
* • **Country Dance** PRE

Hyslop, Ricky
Bow Ties FHM
* • **Broken Baroque**
• **Coastin'**
• **The River**

Jaque, Rhené
• **Daussila** BER

Jenkinson, Ezra
• **Elfentanz (Danse des sylphes)** BOS

Kabalevsky, Dmitri
Thirty Children's Pieces, op. 27 PET
• **Scherzo** (arr. K. Sorokin, in *Kabalevsky: Albumstücke* PET)

Kreisler, Fritz
Four Pieces for Violin and Piano MAS
* • **Toy Soldiers' March**

Kymlicka, Milan
• **Two Dances** CAN
→ no. 2

Massenet, Jules
* • **Invocation (Mélodie)**, from *Les Erinnyes* FIS

Norton, Christopher
Microjazz for Violin B&H
* • **Snow Dance**

Rameau, Jean-Philippe
* • **Two Rigaudons** (arr. from *Pièces de clavecin* FHM)

Shostakovich, Dmitri
* • **Dance** (arr. Konstantin Fortunatow in *Shostakovich: Albumstücke* PET)

Warner, H.E.
• **Perpetuum mobile,** op. 60, no. 3 AUG

Woof, Rowsby
• **Hornpipe** ABR

TECHNICAL REQUIREMENTS

Please see "Technical Requirements" on p. 19 for important information regarding this section of the examination.

Studies/Etudes

Candidates should be prepared to play *two* contrasting selections by different composers from the following list. Compositions marked with an asterisk (*) are included in *Violin Series, Third Edition: Violin Technique 5–8* (Mississauga, Ontario: Frederick Harris Music, 2006). Each bulleted item (•) represents one selection for examination purposes.

Cohen, Mary
Technique Takes Off FAB
* • **Looping the Loop**

Kayser, Heinrich Ernst
Elementary and Progressive Studies for the Violin, op. 20 SCH; FIS
• ***one* of nos. *5, 6, 8**

Sitt, Hans
Studies for the Violin, op. 32, 1 FIS
• ***one* of nos. 8–12**

Trott, Josephine
Melodious Double Stops, 1 SCH
• ***one* of nos. 10–18** (*10)

Wohlfahrt, Franz
60 Studies, op. 45, 2 SCH
• ***one* of nos. *42, 44, 45**

Technical Tests

Please see "Technical Tests" on p. 19 for important information regarding this section of the examination.

Scales, Arpeggios, Broken Intervals, and Double Stops

Please note that all scales, arpeggios, and double stops must be played from memory. Please refer to *Violin Series, Third Edition: Violin Technique 5–8* for required patterns.

Scales	Keys	Range	Tempo	Bowing
Major	D♭, E, F	2 octaves	♩ = 88	
Melodic minor Harmonic minor	C♯, E, F			
Major	C	1 octave *on A string*	♩ = 84	
Chromatic on	G, A	2 octaves	♩ = 76	
Arpeggios				
Major	D♭, E, F	2 octaves	♩ = 120	
Minor	C♯, E, F			
Major	C	1 octave *on A string*	♩ = 84	
Dominant 7th of C major D major	*(starting on G)* *(starting on A)*	2 octaves	♩ = 104	
Diminished 7th of A♭ minor B♭ minor	*(starting on G)* *(starting on A)*			
Broken Intervals and Double Stops				
in 3rds, 6ths, 8ves Major	G, A	1 octave	♩ = 72	

EAR TESTS

Rhythm

Candidates will be asked to sing, clap, or tap the rhythm of a short melody after it has been played *twice* by the examiner.

– *time signatures:* $\frac{3}{4}$ or $\frac{6}{8}$

Intervals

Candidates may choose to:
(a) sing or hum any of the following intervals after the examiner has played the first note *once*, OR
(b) identify any of the following intervals after the examiner has played the interval *once* in broken form.
– *above a given note*: major and minor 3rds and 6ths, perfect 4th, 5th, and octave
– *below a given note*: major and minor 3rds, perfect 5th, and octave

Melody Playback

Candidates will be asked to play back a melody of approximately seven notes, either on the violin or on the piano. The melody will be based on the first five notes and the upper tonic of a major scale. The examiner will name the key, play the tonic triad *once*, and play the melody *twice*.
– *beginning notes*: tonic, mediant, or dominant
– *keys*: G, D, A, or E major

SIGHT READING

1. Candidates will be asked to play a short melody which may contain easy changes of position, approximately equal in difficulty to repertoire of a Grade 3 level.
2. Candidates will be asked to clap or tap the rhythm of a melody in $\frac{3}{4}$ or $\frac{4}{4}$ time. A steady pace and rhythmic accentuation are expected.

THEORY CO-REQUISITES

Preliminary Rudiments

Grade 6

REPERTOIRE

Please see "Examination Repertoire" on pp. 12–13 for important information regarding this section of the examination.

Candidates should be prepared to play *three* contrasting selections: one from List A, one from List B, and one from List C.

- List A includes concertos and *airs variés.*
- List B includes sonatas and sonatinas.
- List C includes concert pieces.

Each bulleted item (•) represents one selection for examination purposes. Compositions marked with an asterisk (*) are included in *Violin Series, Third Edition: Repertoire 6* (Mississauga, Ontario: Frederick Harris Music, 2006). Please note that the selections in List B need not be memorized.

LIST A

Dancla, Charles
Airs variés, op. 89 FIS; SCH
• **no. 4 on a theme by Danzetti**
• **no. 6 on a theme by Mercadante**

Kymlicka, Milan
• **Concertino Grosso** CAN
→ *1st and *3rd movements

Portnoff, Leo
• **Concertino in A minor**, op. 14 BOS
→ 1st movement

Rieding, Oskar
• **Concertino in A minor**, op. 14 BOS
→ 1st movement to *Andante sostenuto*
• **Concerto in G major**, op. 24 BOS
→ *3rd movement

Seitz, Friedrich
• **Concerto in D major**, op. 7 BOS
→ 1st *or* 3rd movement
• **Concerto no. 5 in D major**, op. 22 (in *Suzuki Violin School,* 4 SUM)
→ 3rd movement

Telemann, Georg Philipp
• **Concerto in G major**, op. 3, no. 3 (Schroeder/Kuebart) PET
→ 1st movement

Vivaldi, Antonio
• **Concerto in A minor**, op. 3, no. 6 RV 356/F1:176 (in *Suzuki Violin School,* 4 SUM)
→ 1st *or* 3rd movement

LIST B

Arne, Thomas A.
* • **Sonata no. 5 in B flat major** (transc. Harold Craxton OUP)

Handel, George Frideric
• **Sonata no. 3 in F major**, HWV 370 HEN; PET (in *Suzuki Violin School,* 6 SUM)
→ *two* contrasting movements

Martinů, Bohuslav
• **Sonatina** BAR
→ *2nd *and* *3rd movements

Pepusch, Johann Christoph
Six Kammersonaten LEE; OTT
• **Sonata no. 1 in B minor**
→ *two* contrasting movements
• **Sonata no. 4 in D minor**
→ *two* contrasting movements
• **Sonata no. 6 in F minor**
→ *two* contrasting movements

Telemann, Georg Philipp
Six Sonatas (1715) OTT
• **Sonata no. 1 in G minor**, TWV 41:g1
→ *two* contrasting movements
• **Sonata no. 2 in D major**, TWV 41:D1
→ *two* contrasting movements
• **Sonata no. 3 in B minor**, TWV 41:b1
→ *two* contrasting movements
• **Sonata no. 4 in G major**, TWV 41:G1
→ *two* contrasting movements
• **Sonata no. 5 in A minor**, TWV 41:a1
→ *two* contrasting movements
• **Sonata no. 6 in B minor**, TWV 41:b1
→ *two* contrasting movements

Willan, Healey
• **Sonata no. 2** BOS
→ Largo *and* Courante

LIST C

Baxter, Timothy
* • **Jota** ABR

Bohm, Carl
• **Perpetuum mobile**, from *Little Suite* FIS

Bonporti, Francesco Antonio
Invenzioni da camera, op. 10
* • **Invention in B flat major**, op. 10, no. 5 (arr. Kathleen Wood FHM)

Borowski, Felix
* • **Adoration** PRE

Coulthard, Jean
* • **Rustic Dance**, from *Little French Suite* (in *Encore*, 6 FHM)

Coutts, George
* • **Hornpipe** FHM

Cui, César
Kaleidoscope, op. 50
* • **Musette** (no. 3)

Dolin, Samuel
• **Little Sombrero** BER

Donizetti, Gaetano
• **Non giova il sospirar** (arr. Charles-Auguste de Bériot, in *Romantic Violinist* B&H)

Drdla, František
• **Tarantella**, op. 27, no. 2 BOS

Ethridge, Jean
• **Rondo brillante** (in *Encore*, 4 FHM)

Fauré, Gabriel
• **Berceuse**, op. 16 (in *Solos for the Violin Player* SCH)

Grainger, Percy
• **Molly on the Shore** MAS

Hyslop, Ricky
Bow Ties FHM
• **Sausalito**
String Knots FHM
* • **España**

Kreisler, Fritz
• **Andantino in the Style of Martini** FOL
• **Chanson Louis XIII et Pavane** FOL
Four Pieces for Violin and Piano
* • **Aucassin und Nicolette** MAS

Mollenhauer, Eduard
• **The Boy Paganini** FIS

Oyer, Kathryn
• **Paganini Variations** (in *What's New*, 3 OUP)

Polson, Arthur
• **A Dream** CMC

Potstock, William H.
* • **Souvenir de Sarasate** FIS

Raff, Joseph J.
• **Cavatina**, op. 85, no. 3 EMB

Reger, Max
* • **Romance**

Thornton, Gerry
• **Evening Song** RCM

TECHNICAL REQUIREMENTS

Please see "Technical Requirements" on p. 19 for important information regarding this section of the examination.

Studies/Etudes

Candidates should be prepared to play *two* contrasting selections by different composers from the following list. Compositions marked with an asterisk (*) are included in *Violin Series, Third Edition: Violin Technique 5–8* (Mississauga, Ontario: Frederick Harris Music, 2006). Each bulleted item (•) represents one selection for examination purposes.

Kreutzer, Rodolphe
42 Études ou caprices INT
• **one of nos. *2, 3, 5, 6**

Mazas, Jacques-Féréol
75 Melodious and Progressive Studies / Études spéciales, op. 36, 2 SCH; INT
• **one of nos. *2** (The Sweeping Stroke), **3, 5, 6, 10**

Trott, Josephine
Melodious Double Stops, 1 SCH
• **one of nos. 19–30** (*23)

Wohlfahrt, Franz
* • **Study in G major**, op. 45, no. 50 (in *60 Studies* SCH)

Technical Tests

Please see "Technical Tests" on p. 19 for important information regarding this section of the examination.

Scales, Arpeggios, and Double Stops

Please note that all scales, arpeggios, and double stops must be played from memory. Please refer to *Violin Series, Third Edition: Violin Technique 5–8* for required patterns.

Scales	Keys	Range	Tempo	Bowing
Major Melodic minor Harmonic minor	G, A	3 octaves	♩ = 100	
Major Melodic minor Harmonic minor	D	1 octave *on A string*	♩ = 88	
Chromatic on	B♭, B	2 octaves	♩ = 88	
Arpeggios				
Major Minor	G, A	3 octaves	♩. = 54	
Major Minor	D	1 octave *on A string*	♩ = 88	
Dominant 7th of F major G major	 *(starting on C)* *(starting on D)*	2 octaves	♩ = 88	
Diminished 7th of C♯ minor E♭ minor	 *(starting on B♯)* *(starting on D)*			
Double Stops				
in 3rds, 6ths, 8ves Major Melodic minor	G, A	1 octave	♩ = 76	

EAR TESTS

Rhythm

Candidates will be asked to sing, clap, or tap the rhythm of a short melody after it has been played *twice* by the examiner.

– *time signatures*: 2/4, 3/4, or 6/8

Intervals

Candidates may choose to:

(a) sing or hum any of the following intervals after the examiner has played the first note *once*, OR
(b) identify any of the following intervals after the examiner has played the interval *once* in broken form.
- *above a given note*: major 2nd, major and minor 3rds and 6ths, perfect 4th, 5th, and octave
- *below a given note*: major and minor 3rds, minor 6th, perfect 4th, 5th, and octave

Chords

Candidates will be asked to identify any of the following chords after the examiner has played the chord *once* in solid form, close position:
- major and minor triads in root position.

Melody Playback

Candidates will be asked to play back a melody of approximately nine notes, either on the violin or on the piano. The melody will be based on a complete major scale from tonic to tonic, mediant to mediant, or from dominant to dominant. The examiner will name the key, play the tonic triad *once*, and play the melody *twice*.
- *beginning notes:* tonic, mediant, or dominant
- *keys*: G, D, A, or E major

SIGHT READING

1. Candidates will be asked to play a melody not beyond the third position, approximately equal in difficulty to repertoire of a Grade 4 level.
2. Candidates will be asked to clap or tap the rhythm of a short melody in $\frac{3}{4}$ or $\frac{4}{4}$ time. A steady pace and rhythmic accentuation are expected.

THEORY CO-REQUISITES

Grade 1 Rudiments

Grade 7

REPERTOIRE

Please see "Examination Repertoire" on pp. 12–13 for important information regarding this section of the examination.

Candidates should be prepared to play *three* contrasting selections: one from List A, one from List B, and one from List C.

- List A includes concertos and *airs variés.*
- List B includes sonatas and sonatinas.
- List C includes concert pieces.

Each bulleted item (•) represents one selection for examination purposes. Compositions marked with an asterisk (*) are included in *Violin Series, Third Edition: Repertoire 7* (Mississauga, Ontario: Frederick Harris Music, 2006). Please note that the selections in List B need not be memorized.

LIST A

Dancla, Charles
Airs variés, op. 89 OTT
- **no. 3 on a theme by Bellini**
- **no. 5 on a theme by Weigl**

Marcello, Benedetto
- **Concerto in D major** OTT
  → 1st movement

Nardini, Pietro
- **Concerto in E minor** AUG; INT
  → 1st movement

Seitz, Friedrich
- **Concerto in D major**, op. 15 KAL; BOS
  → 1st movement
- **Concerto in G minor**, op. 12 KAL; BOS
  → *1st movement

Sitt, Hans
- **Concertino in A minor**, op. 70 BOS
  → to *Allegretto*

Stamitz, Anton
- **Concerto in G major** OTT
  → *1st movement

Vivaldi, Antonio
- **Concerto in G major**, op. 3, no. 3, RV 310 / F: 1173 PET
  → 1st movement
- **Concerto in G minor**, op. 12, no. 1 RV 317 / F: 1211 OTT; INT (in *Suzuki Violin School,* 5 SUM)
  → 1st movement

LIST B

Anonymous
- **Sonata in D minor** (arr. Hugh J. McLean, in *Musica da Camera,* no. 103 OUP)
  → *two* contrasting movements

Bach, Johann Christian
- **Sonata in D major**, op. 16, no. 1 BRE
  → *two* contrasting movements

Corelli, Arcangelo
12 Sonate, op. 5
- **Sonata no. 1 in D major**
  → *two* contrasting movements
- **Sonata no. 2 in B flat major**
  → *two* contrasting movements
- **Sonata no. 3 in C major**
  → *two* contrasting movements
- **Sonata no. 4 in F major**
  → *two* contrasting movements
- **Sonata no. 5 in G minor**
  → *two* contrasting movements
- **Sonata no. 6 in A major**
  → *two* contrasting movements

Eccles, Henry
- **Sonata in G minor** INT
  → *two* contrasting movements

Handel, George Frideric
- **Sonata no. 2 in G minor**, HWV 368 HEN; PET
  → *two* contrasting movements
- **Sonata no. 4 in D major**, HWV 371 HEN; PET
  → *two* contrasting movements
- **Sonata no. 6 in E major**, HWV 373 HEN; PET
  → *two* contrasting movements

Haydn, Franz Joseph
- **Sonata no. 6 in C major** (arr. by Haydn from Divertimento in C major, Hob. II:11 SCH; PET)

Mozart, Wolfgang Amadeus
- **Sonata in E minor**, K 304 HEN
  → *1st movement

Schubert, Franz
- **Sonatina in D major**, op. posth. 137, no. 1, D 384 HEN
  → *two* contrasting movements

Vivaldi, Antonio
- **Sonata in F major**, op. 2, no. 4, RV 20; F XIII 32
  → *1st *and* *2nd movements

Weber, Carl Maria von
- **Sonatas**, op. 10b HEN
  → *two* contrasting movements from one sonata

LIST C

Bach, Johann Sebastian
* * • **Adagio in G major** (arr. Kathleen Wood from Cantata no. 156, BWV 1056 FHM)

Barnes, Milton
* • **Three Folk Dances** CMC
  → *no. 3

Bartók, Béla
* * • **Evening in the Country**, from *Ten Easy Pieces* (transc. Tibor Fülep EMB)

Beethoven, Ludwig van
* * • **Variations on a Theme by Paisiello** (arr. Yaakov Geringas from WoO 70)

Bohm, Carl
* • **Introduction and Polonaise** FIS

Brahms, Johannes
* • **Hungarian Dance no. 2** (arr. Paul Klengel, from Hungarian Dances, WoO1, in *Solos for the Violin Player* SCH)

Corelli, Arcangelo
* • **Sarabande and Allegretto** (arr. Fritz Kreisler FOL)

Cui, César
Kaleidoscope, op. 50
* • **Perpetuum mobile**
* * • **Scherzetto** (no. 22)

Ernst, Heinrich W.
* • **Gypsy Dance** FIS

Farmer, Henry
* • **Hope Told a Flattering Tale** (in *Romantic Violinist* B&H)

Fiocco, Joseph Hector
* • **Allegro** [in G major] OTT; INT

Gluck, Christoph Willibald
* • **Mélodie** (*Dance of the Blessed Spirits),* from *Orfeo ed Euridice* (arr. Fritz Kreisler OTT)

Gratton, Hector
* • **Première danse canadienne** CMC

Heuberger, Richard
* • **Midnight Bells** (arr. Fritz Kreisler from *Opera Ball* FOL)

Hubay, Jenö
* • **Bolero** BOS

Hyslop, Ricky
Bow Ties FHM
* • **Haifa**

Järnefeldt, Armas
* • **Berceuse** CHS

Kreisler, Fritz
* • **Liebesleid** FOL
* • **Menuet in the Style of Porpora** FOL

Kreisler, Fritz (continued)
* • **Rondino on a Theme by Beethoven** FOL

Kunits, Luigi von
* • **Scotch Lullaby**

Mascagni, Pietro
* • **Intermezzo sinfonico**, from *Cavalleria rusticana* (arr. FIS; SCH)

Massenet, Jules
* • **Méditation**, from *Thaïs* UMU

Mlynarski, Emil
* • **Mazurka** (in *Solos for Young Violinists* SUM)

Mondonville, Jean-Joseph Cassanéa de
* • **Sonata no. 3 in G major** (in *Solos for the Violin Player* SCH)
  → *Tambourin (4th movement)

Paradis, Maria Theresia von
* • **Sicilienne** OTT

Prokofiev, Sergei
* • **Evening**, from *Children's Suite,* op. 65
* * • **Gavotte** (arr. from Symphony No. 1 in D major, "Classical," op. 25 FHM)

Rebel, Jean-Féry
* • **The Bells** (in *Solos for the Violin Player* SCH)

Severn, Edmund
* • **Polish Dance** FIS

Shostakovich, Dmitri
* * • **Spring Waltz**, op. 27, no. 6 (arr. Konstantin Fortunatov, in *Shostakovich: Albumstücke* PET)

Tchaikovsky, Pyotr Il'yich
* • **Valse sentimentale** (arr. David Grunes from *Six morceaux,* op. 51 OME)

Toselli, Enrico
* • **Serenade,** op. 6 (arr. Fredric Fradkin BMC)

Valdez, Charles Robert
* • **Sérénade du tzigane** FIS

Vaughan Williams, Ralph
* • **Fantasia on Greensleeves** (arr. Michael Mullinar from *Sir John in Love* OUP)

Veracini, Francesco Maria
* • **Gigue from Sonata in D minor** (in *Suzuki Violin School,* 5 SUM)

Weber, Carl Maria von
* • **Country Dance** (in *Suzuki Violin School,* 5 SUM)

Weisgarber, Elliott
* • **The Surface of the Water at Misaka**, from *Six Miniatures after Hokusai* CMC

Wieniawski, Henryk
* • **Kujawiak (Mazurka)** EMB
* • **Mazurka "Le ménétrier,"** op. 19, no. 2 EMB

ORCHESTRAL EXCERPTS

Candidates should be prepared to play *one* excerpt from the following list. Candidates should prepare the first violin part. In addition, candidates are encouraged to listen to and be familiar with the works from which these excerpts are taken.

- All orchestral excerpts are included in *Violin Series, Third Edition: Orchestral Excerpts* (Mississauga, Ontario: Frederick Harris Music, 2006).
- Alternatively, candidates may use standard published orchestral parts for the specific excerpts. The listings below include measure numbers and a suggested publisher for each excerpt.

Bach, Johann Sebastian
• **Brandenburg Concerto No. 3 in G major**, BWV 1048 BRD; KAL
→ 1st movement: mm. 1–8; 39 (beat 4)–54; 78–97 (beat 3)

Beethoven, Ludwig van
• **Symphony No. 7 in A major**, op. 92 BAR
→ 1st movement: mm. 7–23
→ 2nd movement (*Allegretto*): mm. 51–100

Bizet, George
• **Carmen Suite No. 1** BRD
→ no. 5, *Les toréadors*: mm. 1–101 (first eighth note)

Haydn, Franz Joseph
• **Symphony No. 49 in F minor** ("La passione") DBL
→ 2nd movement: mm. 1–51

Mendelssohn, Felix
• **Symphony No. 4 in A major** ("Italian") BRE
→ 3rd movement: mm. 1–40; 63–82

Mozart, Wolfgang Amadeus
• **Symphony No. 29 in A major**, K 201 BAR; BRD
→ 1st movement: mm. 1–77 (beat 2)

Wagner, Richard
• ***Die Meistersinger von Nürnberg*** BRE
Overture: mm. 1–27; 97–108; 196–197

TECHNICAL REQUIREMENTS

Please see "Technical Requirements" on p. 19 for important information regarding this section of the examination.

Studies/Etudes

Candidates should be prepared to play *two* contrasting selections by different composers from the following list. Compositions marked with an asterisk (*) are included in *Violin Series, Third Edition: Violin Technique 5–8* (Mississauga, Ontario: Frederick Harris Music, 2006). Each bulleted item (•) represents one selection for examination purposes.

Dont, Jacob
24 Exercises, op. 37 INT; SCH
• ***one* of nos. 1–7** (*3)

Kreutzer, Rodolphe
42 Études ou caprices INT
• ***one* of nos. 4, *7, 8, 9, 11, 13**

Mazas, Jacques-Féréol
75 Melodious and Progressive Studies / Études spéciales, op. 36, 2 SCH; INT
• ***one* of nos. *8** (Division of the Bow in the *Cantilena*), **9, 17, 21**

Polo, Enrico
30 Studi a corde doppie RIC
* • **no. 23**

Technical Tests

Please see "Technical Tests" on p. 19 for important information regarding this section of the examination.

Scales, Arpeggios, and Double Stops

Please note that all scales, arpeggios, and double stops must be played from memory. Please refer to *Violin Series, Third Edition: Violin Technique 5–8* for required patterns.

TECHNICAL REQUIREMENTS continued

Scales	Keys	Range	Tempo	Bowing
Major	A♭, B♭, C	3 octaves	♩ = 120	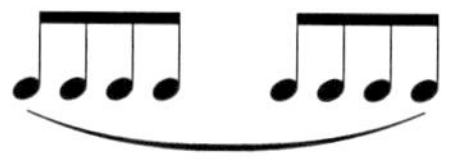 (Galamian Pattern)
Melodic minor Harmonic minor	G♯, B♭, C			
Artificial Harmonics Major	G	1 octave	♩ = 80	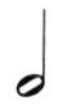
Chromatic on	C, D	2 octaves	♩ = 108	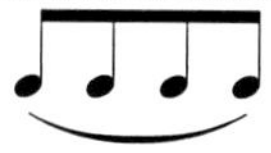
Arpeggios				
Major	A♭, B♭, C	3 octaves	♩. = 72	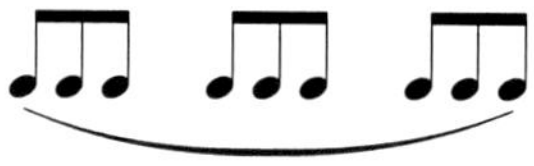
Minor	G♯, B♭, C			
Dominant 7th of C major D major E♭ major	 *(starting on G)* *(starting on A)* *(starting on B♭)*	3 octaves	♩ = 100	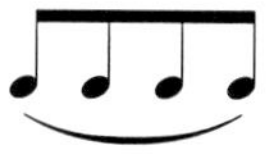
Diminished 7th of A♭ minor B♭ minor B minor	 *(starting on G)* *(starting on A)* *(starting on A♯)*			
Double Stops				
in 3rds, 6ths, 8ves Major Minor	B♭, C	1 octave	♩ = 92	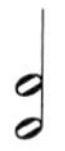

EAR TESTS

Rhythm

Candidates will be asked to sing, clap, or tap the rhythm of a short melody after it has been played *twice* by the examiner.

– *time signatures*: $\frac{2}{4}$, $\frac{3}{4}$, or $\frac{6}{8}$

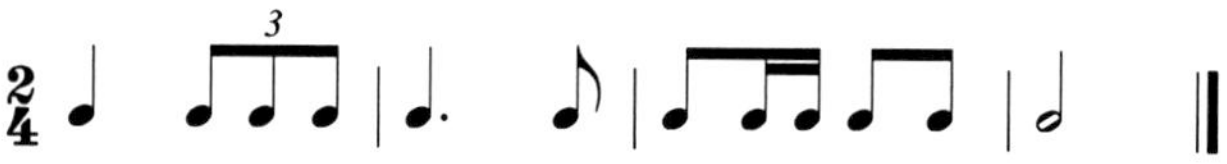

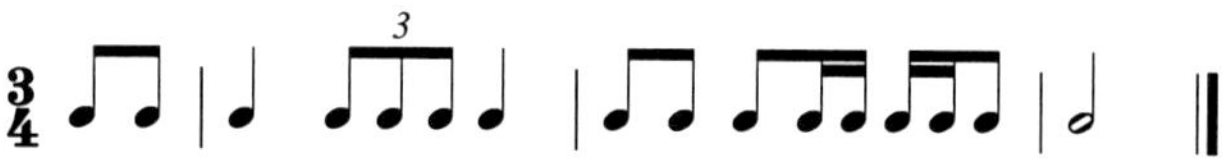

Intervals

Candidates may choose to:

(a) sing or hum any of the following intervals after the examiner has played the first note *once*, OR
(b) identify any of the following intervals after the examiner has played the interval *once* in broken form.
– *above a given note*: major and minor 2nds, 3rds, and 6ths, perfect 4th, 5th, and octave
– *below a given note*: major and minor 3rds, minor 6th, major 7th, perfect 4th, 5th, and octave

Chords

Candidates will be asked to identify any of the following chords after the examiner has played the chord *once* in solid form, close position:

– major and minor triads in root position.
– dominant 7th chords in root position.

Melody Playback

Candidates will be asked to play back a melody of approximately nine notes, either on the violin or on the piano. The melody will be based on a complete major scale from tonic to tonic, mediant to mediant, or from dominant to dominant. The examiner will name the key, play the tonic triad *once*, and play the melody *twice*.

– *beginning notes*: tonic, mediant, dominant, or upper tonic
– *keys*: C, G, D, A, or E major

SIGHT READING

1. Candidates will be asked to play a short composition equal in difficulty to repertoire of a Grade 5 level.
2. Candidates will be asked to clap or tap the rhythm of a short melody in $\frac{2}{4}$ or $\frac{6}{8}$ time. A steady pace and rhythmic accentuation are expected.

THEORY CO-REQUISITES

Grade 2 Rudiments

Grade 8

REPERTOIRE

Please see "Examination Repertoire" on pp. 12–13 for important information regarding this section of the examination.

Candidates should be prepared to play *four* contrasting selections: one from List A, one from List B, one from List C, and one from List D.

- List A includes concertos and *airs variés*.
- List B includes sonatas and sonatinas.
- List C includes concert pieces.
- List D includes unaccompanied works.

Each bulleted item (•) represents one selection for examination purposes. Compositions marked with an asterisk (*) are included in *Violin Series, Third Edition: Repertoire 8* (Mississauga, Ontario: Frederick Harris Music, 2006). Please note that the selections in List B need not be memorized.

LIST A

Accolay, Jean-Baptiste
- **Concerto in A minor**, op. 12 FIS; INT

Bach, Johann Sebastian
- **Concerto in A minor**, BWV 1041 INT
  → 1st movement

Benda, Johann
- **Concerto in G major** (arr. Samuel Dushkin OTT)
  → 1st movement

Dancla, Charles
Airs variés, op. 118 FIS
- **no. 1: I Montecchi e I Capuletti**
- **no. 2: La Straniera**
- **no. 3: Norma**
- **no. 4: La Sonnambula**
- **no. 5: Les Puritains**
- **no. 6: Le Carnaval de Venise**

de Bériot, Charles-Auguste
- **Concerto in B minor**, op. 32 PET
  → 1st movement

Haydn, Franz Joseph
- **Concerto in G major**, Hob. VIIa: 4 HEN; PET
  → *1st movement with cadenza

Komarowski, Anatoli
- **Concerto no. 1 in E minor** PET
  → *1st movement

Kreisler, Fritz
- **Concerto in C major**, in the style of Vivaldi FOL
  → 1st *and* 2nd movements

Rieding, Oskar
- **Concerto in E minor**, op. 7 BOS
  → 1st movement to page 3, line 3

LIST B

Albinoni, Tomaso
- **Sonata in A major**, op. 6, no. 11 NAG
  → *two* contrasting movements
- **Sonata in D major**, op. 6, no. 7
  → *two* contrasting movements
- **Sonata in G minor**, op. 6, no. 2 OTT
  → *two* contrasting movements

Bartók, Béla
- **Sonatina** (transc. André Gertler EMB)
  → *I. Bagpipers *and* *II. Bear Dance

Dvořák, Antonín
- **Sonatina in G major**, op. 100 FIS
  → *two* contrasting movements

Handel, George Frideric
- **Sonata no. 1 in A major**, HWV 361 HEN; PET
  → *two* contrasting movements
- **Sonata no. 5 in A major**, HWV 372 HEN; PET
  → *two* contrasting movements

Mozart, Wolfgang Amadeus
- **Sonata in G major**, K 293a (301) HEN
  → 1st *or* 2nd movement

Schubert, Franz
- **Sonatina in A minor**, op. posth. 137, no. 2, D 385 HEN
  → *1st *and* *2nd movements
- **Sonatina in G minor**, op. posth. 137, no. 3, D 408 HEN
  → *two* contrasting movements

Tartini, Giuseppe
Sonatas, op. 1
- ***one* sonata** (except Sonata no. 9 or Sonata no. 10)
  → *two* contrasting movements

Sonatas, op. 2
- ***one* sonata**
  → *two* contrasting movements

Vivaldi, Antonio
- **Sonata in D minor**, op. 2, no. 3, RV 14/F XII 31 INT
  → *two* contrasting movements

LIST C

Albeniz, Isaac
- **Tango** (arr. Fritz Kreisler FOL)

Bach, Johann Sebastian
- **Air on the G String** (arr. August Wilhelmj from Orchestral Suite no. 3 in D major, BWV 1068 FIS; RIC)

Boulanger, Lili
Deux morceaux SCH
- **Cortège**
- **Nocturne** (in *Frauen Komponieren* OTT)

Champagne, Claude
- **Danse villageoise** BER; CMC

Dahlgren, David
* • **Scherzo**

d'Ambrosio, Alfredo
- **Canzonetta** (in *Romantic Violinist* B&H)

Debussy, Claude
- **La fille aux cheveux de lin** (transc. Arthur Hartmann DUR)

Have, Willem ten
* • **Allegro brillant**, op. 19 FIS

Healey, Derek E.
Six Epigrams ECK
* • **nos. 2, 5, *and* 6**

Hyslop, Ricky
Bow Ties FHM
- **The Red Shoes**
- **Released**

Jaque, Rhené
- **Petit air roumain** CMC
- **Spiccato e legato**

Kolinski, Mieczyslaw
- **Little Suite** CMC
  → *two* contrasting movements

Kreisler, Fritz
- **La gitana** FOL
- **Liebesfreud** FOL
- **Schön Rosmarin** FOL
- **Sicilienne and Rigaudon in the Style of Francoeur** FOL; OTT

Kulesha, Gary
- **Song and Dance** CMC
  → *Dance

Monti, Vittorio
- **Csárdás** RIC; FIS

Mozart, Wolfgang Amadeus
- **Minuet** (arr. from String Quartet in D minor, K 421, in *Suzuki Violin School,* 7 SUM)
- **Rondo in D major**, K 485 (in *Solos for the Violin Player* SCH)

Mussorgsky, Modest
* • **Hopak** (arr. Sergei Rachmaninoff)

Perrault, Michel Brunet
* • **Solitude**

Ries, Franz Anton
- **Perpetuum mobile**, op. 34, no. 5 FIS

Sarasate, Pablo de
- **Playera** (*Spanish Dance,* op. 23, no. 5, in *Romantic Violinist* B&H)

Schubert, Franz
- **Die Biene/The Bee**, op. 13, no. 9

Senaillé, Jean-Baptiste
* • **Les polichinelles** (arr. Alfred Moffat OTT)

Shostakovich, Dmitri
- **Romance in C major** (in *Shostakovich: Albumstücke* PET)

Wieniawski, Henryk
- **Mazurka "Obertass,"** op. 19, no. 1 MAS

LIST D

Bach, Johann Sebastian
- **Partita no. 2 in D minor**, BWV 1004 BAR; HEN
  → Giga
- **Partita no. 3 in E major**, BWV 1006 BAR; HEN
  → *V. Bourrée *or* *VI. Gigue

Telemann, Georg Philipp
Twelve Fantasias for Violin BAR; INT
- **Fantasia no. 1 in B flat major**, TWV 40:14
  → Largo *or* Allegro
- **Fantasia no. 7 in E flat major**, TWV 40:20
  → Allegro
- **Fantasia no. 8 in E major**, TWV 40:21
  → Spirituoso
- **Fantasia no. 12 in A minor**, TWV 40:25
  → *Moderato *or* Vivace

ORCHESTRAL EXCERPTS

Candidates should be prepared to play *two* contrasting excerpts from the following list. Candidates should prepare the first violin part. In addition, candidates are encouraged to listen to and be familiar with the works from which these excerpts are taken.

- All orchestral excerpts are included in *Violin Series, Third Edition: Orchestral Excerpts* (Mississauga, Ontario: Frederick Harris Music, 2006).
- Alternatively, candidates may use standard published orchestral parts for the specific excerpts. The listings below include measure numbers and a suggested publisher for each excerpt.

Bach, Johann Sebastian
- **Brandenburg Concerto No. 3 in G major**, BWV 1048 BRD
  → 3rd movement: mm. 1–18 (second eighth note); 24–35 (beat 1)

Beethoven, Ludwig van
- **Symphony No. 2 in D major,** op. 36 BAR
  → 3rd movement: complete

Gershwin, George
- **An American in Paris** NWW
  → mm. 1–59

Haydn, Franz Joseph
- **Symphony No. 94 in G major** ("Surprise"), Hob. I:94 BAR; BRH
  → 2nd movement: mm. 1–24; 49–74; 107–114

Mozart, Wolfgang Amadeus
- **Symphony No. 25 in G minor**, K 183 BAR
  → 1st movement: (*Allegro con brio*): mm. 1–12 (beat 2); 29–83; 192 to end

Saint-Saëns, Camille
- **Symphony No. 3 in C minor,** op. 78 KAL; DUR
  → 1st movement: mm. 12–50; 180–208

Schubert, Franz
- **Symphony No. 5 in B flat major**, D 485 BRH
  → 1st movement: mm. 3–23; 41–64; 120–134

TECHNICAL REQUIREMENTS

Please see "Technical Requirements" on p. 19 for important information regarding this section of the examination.

Studies/Etudes

Candidates should be prepared to play *one* selection from the following list. Compositions marked with an asterisk (*) are included in *Violin Series, Third Edition: Violin Technique 5–8* (Mississauga, Ontario: Frederick Harris Music, 2006). Each bulleted item (•) represents one selection for examination purposes.

Campagnoli, Bartolomeo
7 Divertimenti op. 18 RIC; MAY
- * **Divertimento** no. 2
  → Polonaise *and* Trio

Dont, Jacob
24 Studies/Twenty-four Exercises, op. 37 INT; SCH
- ***one* of nos. 9–12** (*9)

Fiorillo, Federigo
34 Etudes ou Caprices INT; SCH
- ***one* of nos. *3, 6, 14, 16**

Kreutzer, Rodolphe
42 Études ou caprices INT
- ***one* of nos. 10, 12, 14, *15, 16, 17**

Mazas, Jacques-Féréol
75 Melodious and Progressive Studies/Études spéciales, op. 36, 2 SCH; INT
- ***one* of nos. 33, 34, 35, 36, 39**

TECHNICAL REQUIREMENTS

Technical Tests

Please see "Technical Tests" on p. 19 for important information regarding this section of the examination.

Scales, Arpeggios, and Double Stops

Please note that all scales, arpeggios, and double stops must be played from memory. Please refer to *Violin Series, Third Edition: Violin Technique 5–8* for required patterns.

Scales	Keys	Range	Tempo	Bowing
Major	B, D♭, D	3 octaves	♩ = 138	 ♩♩♩♩ ♩♩♩♩ (slurred) (Galamian Pattern)
Melodic minor Harmonic minor	B, C♯, D			
Artificial Harmonics Major	A, B♭	1 octave	♩ = 108	 𝅗𝅥
Chromatic on	G, A, B♭	3 octaves	♩ = 120	 ♩♩♩♩ ♩♩♩♩ ♩♩♩♩ (slurred)
Arpeggios				
Major	B, D♭, D	3 octaves	♩. = 84	 ♩♩♩ ♩♩♩ ♩♩♩ (slurred)
Minor	B, C♯, D			
Dominant 7th of D♭ major E major F major	 *(starting on A♭)* *(starting on B)* *(starting on C)*	3 octaves	♩ = 108	 ♩♩♩♩ (slurred)
Diminished 7th of A minor C minor C♯ minor	 *(starting on G♯)* *(starting on B)* *(starting on B♯)*			
Double Stops				
in 3rds, 6ths, 8ves Major Melodic minor	G, A	2 octaves	♩ = 72	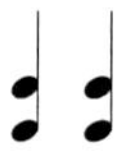 ♩ ♩ (double stops)
in 3rds, 6ths, 8ves Harmonic minor	G, A	1 octave		

EAR TESTS

Intervals

Candidates may choose to:

(a) sing or hum any of the following intervals after the examiner has played the first note *once*, OR
(b) identify any of the following intervals after the examiner has played the interval *once* in broken form.
  – *above a given note*: major and minor 2nds, 3rds, and 6ths, minor 7th, perfect 4th, 5th, and octave
  – *below a given note*: major 2nd, major and minor 3rds, minor 6th, major 7th, perfect 4th, 5th, and octave

Chords

Candidates will be asked to identify any of the following chords after the examiner has played the chord *once* in solid form, close position:

- major and minor triads in root position.
- dominant 7th and diminished 7th chords in root position.

Cadences

Candidates will be asked to identify, by name or symbols, any of the following cadences in major or minor keys. The examiner will play the tonic chord *once*, and then play a short phrase ending with a cadence *twice*.

- perfect (authentic, V–I)
- plagal (IV–I)

Melody Playback

Candidates will be asked to play back a melody of approximately nine notes, either on the violin or on the piano. The melody will be about an octave in range and will contain rhythmic figures that are slightly more difficult than those used for the rhythmic test for Grade 6. The examiner will name the key, play the tonic triad *once*, and play the melody *twice*.

- keys: C, G, D, A, or E major

Sight Reading

1. Candidates will be asked to play a short composition equal in difficulty to repertoire of a Grade 6 level.
2. Candidates will be asked to sing, clap, or tap the rhythm of a melody in $\frac{3}{4}$ or $\frac{6}{8}$ time. A steady pace and rhythmic accentuation are expected.

THEORY CO-REQUISITES

Grade 2 Rudiments
Introductory Harmony (optional)

Grade 9

REPERTOIRE

Please see "Examination Repertoire" on pp. 12–13 for important information regarding this section of the examination.

Candidates should be prepared to play *four* contrasting selections: one from List A, one from List B, one from List C, and one from List D.

- List A includes concertos.
- List B includes sonatas and sonatinas.
- List C includes concert pieces.
- List D consists of unaccompanied works by Johann Sebastian Bach.

Each bulleted item (•) represents one selection for examination purposes. Unless otherwise indicated, candidates should prepare the complete work. Please note that the selections in List B need not be memorized.

LIST A

Bach, Johann Sebastian
- **Concerto in E major**, BWV 1042 INT
  → 1st *and* 2nd movements

Bériot, Charles-Auguste de
- **Concerto in D major**, op. 16 PET
  → 1st movement (to first *tutti*)
- **Concerto in G major**, op. 76, no. 7 FIS
  → 1st movement *and* 2nd movement (to *Allegro moderato*)
- **Concerto in A minor**, op. 104 PET
  → 1st *and* 2nd movements

Haydn, Franz Joseph
- **Concerto in C major**, Hob. VIIa: 1 HEN; PET
  → 1st *and* 2nd movements, with cadenzas

Kreutzer, Rodolphe
- **Concerto in D major**, no. 13 FIS
  → 1st *and* 2nd movements

Mozart, Wolfgang Amadeus
- **Concerto in B flat major**, K 207 BAR; PET; INT
  → 1st *and* 2nd movements, with cadenzas
- **Concerto in D major**, K 211 BAR; PET; INT
  → 1st *and* 2nd movements, with cadenzas
- **Concerto in G major**, K 216 BAR; PET; INT
  → 1st *and* 2nd movements, with cadenzas

Rode, Pierre
- **Concerto no. 7 in A minor**, op. 9 SCH; INT
  → 1st *and* 2nd movements, with cadenza
- **Concerto no. 8 in E minor**, op. 13 SCH
  → 1st *and* 2nd movements

Viotti, Giovanni Battista
- **Concerto in G major**, no. 23 PET
  → 1st *and* 2nd movements, with cadenza

LIST B

Adaskin, Murray
- **Sonatine baroque** for solo violin RIC
  → 3rd movement

Beethoven, Ludwig van
- **Sonata in D major**, op. 12, no. 1 HEN
  → 1st movement
- **Sonata in A major**, op. 12, no. 2 HEN
  → 1st movement
- **Sonata in F major** ("Spring"), op. 24 HEN
  → 1st movement

Hindemith, Paul
- **Sonata in E flat**, op. 11, no. 1 OTT
  → 1st movement

Leclair, Jean Marie
- **Sonata in D major**, op. 9 SCH
  → *two* contrasting movements

Mozart, Wolfgang Amadeus
- **Sonata in C major**, K 296 HEN
  → 1st movement

Mozart, Wolfgang Amadeus (continued)
- **Sonata in F major**, K 374d (376) HEN
  → 1st movement
- **Sonata in F major**, K 374e (377) HEN
  → 1st movement

Tartini, Giuseppe
- **Sonata in G minor** ("Didone Abbandonata") SCH; RIC
  → 1st *and* 2nd movements

Veracini, Francesco Maria
- **Sonata in E minor** INT; RIC
  → 1st *and* 2nd movements

Vivaldi, Antonio
- **Sonata in D major**, RV 10/F XII 6 (transc. Ottorino Respighi RIC)
  → *two* contrasting movements

Willan, Healey
- **Sonata no. 1 in E minor** BER
  → 1st movement

LIST C

Albeniz, Isaac
- **Malagueña** (arr. Fritz Kreisler FOL)
- **Mallorca**, from *Three Spanish Dances* MAS
- **Tango in D major**, op. 165, no. 2 (arr. Samuel Dushkin OTT)

Bacewicz, Grazina
- **Humoreska** (in *Frauen Komponieren* OTT)
- **Polish Caprice** for violin solo PWM

Barber, Samuel
- **Canzone**, op. 38 SCH

Beethoven, Ludwig van
- **Romance in F major**, op. 50 SCH

Debussy, Claude
- **La plus que lent** (arr. Leon Rocques DUR)

Dvořák, Antonín
- **Romantic Pieces**, op. 75 HEN
  → *two* pieces
- **Slavonic Dance no. 2 in E minor** (arr. Fritz Kreisler FOL)
- **Slavonic Dance no. 3 in G major** (arr. Fritz Kreisler FOL)

Eckhardt-Gramatté, Sophie-Carmen
Ten Caprices CMC
- **Caprice no. 1**

Gratton, Hector
- **Quatrième danse canadienne** BER [OP]

Holt, Patricia Blomfield
- **Suite no. 2** BER
  → *two* contrasting movements

Hubay, Jenö
- **Hejre Kati**, op. 32 SCH; FIS

Kodály, Zoltán
- **Adagio** EMB; B&H

Kreisler, Fritz
- **The Old Refrain** FOL

Moszkowski, Moritz
Five Spanish Dances, op. 12 PET
- **no. 1**
- **no. 5**

Mozart, Wolfgang Amadeus
- **Rondo in C major**, K 373 INT

Prokofiev, Sergei
- **Gavotta**, op. 32, no. 3 (arr. Jascha Heifetz FIS)

Rachmaninoff, Sergei
- **Vocalise**, op. 34, no. 14 INT

Raminsh, Imant
- **Aria** CMC

Sarasate, Pablo de
- **Malagueña** (*Spanish Dance,* op. 21, no. 1) INT

Schubert, Franz
- **Ave Maria** (arr. August Wilhelmj FIS)

Suk, Joseph
- **Four Pieces**, op. 17 SIM
  → *one* piece

Svendsen, Johan
- **Romance**, op. 26 PET; FIS

Tchaikovsky, Pyotr Il'yich
- **Mélodie**, op. 42, no. 3 FIS; INT

LIST D

Bach, Johann Sebastian
- **Partita no. 1 in B minor**, BWV 1002 BAR; HEN
  → Courante
- **Partita no. 2 in D minor**, BWV 1004 BAR; HEN
  → Allemande *or* Corrente *or* Sarabanda
- **Partita no. 3 in E major**, BWV 1006 BAR; HEN
  → Gavotte en rondeau
- **Sonata no. 3 in C major**, BWV 1005 BAR; HEN
  → Allegro assai
- **Sonata no. 1 in G minor**, BWV 1001 BAR; HEN
  → Adagio

ORCHESTRAL EXCERPTS

Candidates should be prepared to play *two* contrasting excerpts from the following list. Candidates should prepare the first violin part. In addition, candidates are encouraged to listen to and be familiar with the works from which these excerpts are taken.

- All orchestral excerpts are included in *Violin Series, Third Edition: Orchestral Excerpts* (Mississauga, Ontario: Frederick Harris Music, 2006).
- Alternatively, candidates may use standard published orchestral parts for the specific excerpts. The listings below include measure numbers and a suggested publisher for each excerpt.

Beethoven, Ludwig van
- **Symphony No. 1 in C major**, op. 21 BAR
  → 3rd movement (*Minuet and Trio*): complete
  → 4th movement (*Finale*): mm. 1–86

Brahms, Johannes
- **Symphony No. 1 in C minor**, op. 68 BRH; FIS
  → 1st movement: mm. 1–29; 41–70

Britten, Benjamin
- **The Young Person's Guide to the Orchestra, Variations and Fugue on a theme of Henry Purcell** B&H
  → variation M: mm. 1–54; 64

Dukas, Paul
- **The Sorcerer's Apprentice** KAL
  → mm. 135–198; pickup to 221–293

Haydn, Franz Joseph
- **Symphony No. 104 in D major** ("London") HMP
  → 1st movement: mm. 17–64; 166–192
  → 2nd movement: mm. 1–8; 42–56; pickup to 146–152

Mozart, Wolfgang Amadeus
- **Symphony No. 40 in G minor**, K 550 BRH
  → 1st movement: mm. 1–42; 103–126; 191–225; pickup to 288–299

Rossini, Gioachino
- ***La gazza ladra*** BRH
  → Overture: mm. 3–11; pickup to 42–49; 62–114

TECHNICAL REQUIREMENTS

Please see "Technical Requirements" on p. 19 for important information regarding this section of the examination.

Studies/Etudes

Candidates should be prepared to play *one* selection from the following list. Each bulleted item (•) represents one selection for examination purposes.

Dont, Jacob
24 Studies, op. 37 INT; SCH
- ***one* of nos. 13–24**

Fiorillo, Federigo
34 Etudes or Caprices INT; SCH
- ***one* of nos. 5, 7, 21, 22, 31**

Kreutzer, Rodolphe
42 Études ou caprices INT
- ***one* of nos. 18–26**

Rode, Pierre
24 Caprices FIS; INT
- ***one* of nos. 1, 2, 3, 5, 8, 10**

Technical Tests

Please see "Technical Tests" on p. 19 for important information regarding this section of the examination.

Scales, Arpeggios, and Double Stops

Please note that all scales, arpeggios, and double stops must be played from memory.

Scales	Keys	Range	Tempo	Bowing
Major Melodic minor Harmonic minor	E♭, E, F	3 octaves	♩ = 84	(Galamian Pattern)
Artificial Harmonics Major	G, A	2 octaves	♩ = 84	
Chromatic on	B, C, D	3 octaves	♩ = 72	
Arpeggios				
Major Minor	E♭, E, F	3 octaves	♩. = 92	
Dominant 7th of G♭ major G major A♭ major	*(starting on D♭)* *(starting on D)* *(starting on E♭)*	3 octaves	♩ = 60	
Diminished 7th of D minor E♭ minor E minor	*(starting on C♯)* *(starting on D)* *(starting on D♯)*			
Double Stops				
in 3rds, 6ths, 8ves Major Melodic minor	B, C, D	2 octaves	♩ = 84	
in 3rds, 6ths, 8ves Harmonic minor	B, C, D	1 octave	♩ = 84	

EAR TESTS

Intervals

Candidates may choose to:

(a) sing or hum any of the following intervals after the examiner has played the first note *once*, OR

(b) identify any of the following intervals after the examiner has played the interval *once* in broken form.

- *above a given note*: any interval within the octave
- *below a given note*: any interval within the octave except a diminished 5th (augmented 4th)

Chords

Candidates will be asked to identify any of the following chords after the examiner has played the chord *once* in solid form, close position:

- major and minor triads in root position and first inversion. Candidates must identify the quality of the triad (major or minor) and name the inversion.
- dominant 7th and diminished 7th chords in root position.

Cadences

Candidates will be asked to identify, by name or by symbols, any of the following cadences in major or minor keys. The examiner will play the tonic chord *once*, and then play a short phrase ending with a cadence *twice*.

- perfect (authentic, V–I)
- plagal (IV–I)
- imperfect (I–V)

Melody Playback

Candidates will be asked to play back the *upper* part of a two-part phrase in any major key, either on the violin or on the piano. The examiner will name the key, play the tonic triad *once*, and play the phrase *twice*.

SIGHT READING

1. Candidates will be asked to play a composition approximately equal in difficulty to repertoire of a Grade 7 level.
2. Candidates will be asked to clap or tap the rhythm of a melody in $\frac{3}{4}$ or $\frac{4}{4}$ time. A steady pace and rhythmic accentuation are expected.

THEORY CO-REQUISITES

Grade 2 Rudiments
Grade 3 Harmony *or* Grade 3 Keyboard Harmony
Grade 3 History

Grade 10

Please see "Theory Examinations: Prerequisites and Co-requisites" on p. 7, "ARCT Examinations" on p. 8, "Classification of Marks" on p. 15, and "Supplemental Examinations" on p. 16 for important details regarding Grade 10 standing for an ARCT examination application.

REPERTOIRE

Please see "Examination Repertoire" on pp. 12–13 for important information regarding this section of the examination.

Candidates should be prepared to play *four* contrasting selections: one from List A, one from List B, one from List C, and one from List D.

- List A includes concertos.
- List B includes sonatas.
- List C includes concert pieces.
- List D consists of unaccompanied works by Johann Sebastian Bach.

Each bulleted item (•) represents one selection for examination purposes. Unless otherwise indicated, candidates should prepare the complete work. Please note that the selections in List B need not be memorized.

LIST A

Bruch, Max
- **Concerto in G minor**, op. 26 PET; SCH; INT
  → 1st *and* 2nd movements

Kabalevsky, Dmitri
- **Concerto in C**, op. 48 INT
  → 1st *and* 2nd movements

Mozart, Wolfgang Amadeus
- **Concerto in D major**, K 218 INT
  → 1st *and* 2nd movements, with Joachim's cadenzas

Spohr, Louis
- **Concerto in D minor**, op. 2 PET
  → 1st *and* 2nd movements
- **Concerto in A minor**, op. 47 PET
  → opening to *Allegro moderato OR Allegro moderato* to end
- **Concerto in D minor**, op. 55 PET
  → 1st *and* 2nd movements

Viotti, Giovanni Battista
- **Concerto in A minor**, no. 22 SCH
  → 1st *and* 2nd movements

LIST B

Beethoven, Ludwig van
- **Sonata in E flat major**, op. 12, no. 3 HEN
  → 1st *and* 2nd movements
- **Sonata in A minor**, op. 23 HEN
  → 1st *and* 2nd movements
- **Sonata in A major**, op. 30, no. 1 HEN
  → 1st *and* 2nd movements
- **Sonata in G major**, op. 30, no. 3 HEN
  → 1st *and* 2nd movements
- **Sonata in G major**, op. 96 HEN
  → 1st *and* 2nd movements

Brahms, Johannes
- **Sonata in G major**, op. 78 HEN; INT
  → 1st *and* 2nd movements
- **Sonata in A major**, op. 100 HEN; INT
  → 1st *and* 2nd movements

Buczynski, Walter
- **Sonata 1979** CMC

Girón, Arsenio
- **Sonata breve** CMC
  → 1st *and* 2nd movements *OR* 3rd *and* 4th movements

Grieg, Edvard
- **Sonata in F major**, op. 8, no. 1 PET; SCH
  → 1st *and* 2nd movements
- **Sonata in C minor**, op. 45, no. 3 PET; SCH
  → 1st *and* 2nd movements

Hindemith, Paul
- **Sonata in C** (1939) OTT
  → 1st *and* 2nd movements

Mozart, Wolfgang Amadeus
- **Sonata in E flat major**, K 481 HEN
  → 1st *and* 2nd movements
- **Sonata in A major**, K 526 HEN
  → 1st *and* 2nd movements

Prokofiev, Sergei
- **Sonata**, op. 115 PET

Schubert, Franz
- **Sonata in A major**, op. posth. 162, D 574 HEN; OTT
  → 1st *and* 2nd movements

Schumann, Robert
- **Sonata in A minor**, op. 105 PET
  → 1st *and* 2nd movements

Vallerand, Jean
- **Sonata** (1950) DOM
  → *two* contrasting movements

LIST C

Anonymous
- **Ciaccona in G minor** (erroneously attr. Tomaso Antonio Vitali; arr. Léopold Charlier and Leopold Auer FIS)

Archer, Violet
- **Prelude and Allegro** BER

Bartók, Béla
- **Roumanian Folk Dances** UNI

Beethoven, Ludwig van
- **Romance in G major**, op. 40 HEN

Bloch, Ernest
- **Nigun**, from *Baal Shem* FIS

Brahms, Johannes
- **Hungarian Dances, nos. 1–5** (arr. Joseph Joachim from Hungarian Dances WoO1 FIS)
  → *one* dance

Copland, Aaron
- **Hoe-down**, from *Rodeo* B&H

Debussy, Claude
- **Golliwogg's Cake-walk** (arr. Jascha Heifetz FIS)

Eckhardt-Gramatté, Sophie-Carmen
Ten Caprices CMC
- **no. 2**
- **no. 3**

Elgar, Edward
- **La capricieuse**, op. 17 FIS; BRH

Girón, Arsenio
- **Five Episodes** CMC
  → *three* contrasting movements

Glazunov, Alexander
- **Meditation**, op. 32 SCH

Hyslop, Ricky
Bow Ties FHM
- **L'amour de la jeune fille**

Kreisler, Fritz
- **Praeludium and Allegro in the Style of Pugnani** OTT
- **Variations on a Theme of Corelli** FOL

Kroll, William
- **Banjo and Fiddle** SCH

Moszkowski, Moritz
- **Guitarre**, op. 45, no. 2 FIS; PET

Mozart, Wolfgang Amadeus
- **Rondo in G major** (arr. Fritz Kreisler from *Haffner Serenade,* K 250 FOL)

Nováček, Ottokar
- **Moto perpetuo** INT

Prokofiev, Sergei
- **Five Melodies**, op. 35 bis B&H
- **March** (arr. Jascha Heifetz from *Love for Three Oranges* FIS)

Sarasate, Pablo de
- **Jota de Pablo**, op. 52 SCH
- **Romanza andaluza** (*Spanish Dance,* op. 22) INT

Tchaikovsky, Pyotr Il'yich
- **Scherzo**, op. 42, no. 2 PET
- **Sérénade mélancolique**, op. 26 PET

Webern, Anton von
- **Four Pieces**, op. 7 UNI

Wieniawski, Henryk
- **Légende**, op. 17 FIS

LIST D

Bach, Johann Sebastian
- **Sonata no. 1 in G minor**, BWV 1001 BAR; HEN
  → Siciliana *or* Presto
- **Partita no. 1 in B minor**, BWV 1002 BAR; HEN
  → Allemande and Double *OR* Sarabande and Double *OR* Tempo di bourrée and Double
- **Sonata no. 2 in A minor**, BWV 1003 BAR; HEN
  → Andante *or* Allegro
- **Sonata no. 3 in C major**, BWV 1005 BAR; HEN
  → Adagio *or* Largo
- **Partita no. 3 in E major**, BWV 1006 BAR; HEN
  → Preludio *or* Loure

ORCHESTRAL EXCERPTS

Candidates should be prepared to play *two* contrasting excerpts from the following list. Candidates should prepare the first violin part. In addition, candidates are encouraged to listen to and be familiar with the works from which these excerpts are taken.

- All orchestral excerpts are included in *Violin Series, Third Edition: Orchestral Excerpts* (Mississauga, Ontario: Frederick Harris Music, 2006).
- Alternatively, candidates may use standard published orchestral parts for the specific excerpts. The listings below include measure numbers and a suggested publisher for each excerpt.

Beethoven, Ludwig van
- **Symphony No. 8 in F major,** op. 93 BAR
  → 2nd movement: pickup to 41–81
  → 4th movement: mm. 1–90

Berlioz, Hector
- **Symphonie fantastique;** *épisode de la vie d'un artiste* BRH
  → 1st movement (*Rêveries, passions*): mm. 3–25
  → 2nd movement (*Un bal*): pickup to mm. 39–94; pickup to 257–300, pickup to 346–368

Brahms, Johannes
- **Symphony No. 4 in E minor** BRD; BRH
  → 4th movement: mm. 41–79; 153–177

Debussy, Claude
- ***La mer*** KAL
  → 2nd movement (*Jeux de vagues*): mm. 163–218

Mendelssohn, Felix
- **Symphony No. 4 in A major** ("Italian") BRH
  → 1st movement: mm. 1–110; 187–284

Mozart, Wolfgang Amadeus
- ***Die Zauberflöte*** (The Magic Flute) BAR; BRH
  → Overture: mm. 20–96; 216 to end

Tchaikovsky, Pyotr Il'yich
- **Symphony No. 4 in F minor**, op. 36 BRH; KAL
  → 1st movement: pickup to 70–103; pickup to 237–262
  → 2nd movement: 85–117

Weber, Carl Maria von
- ***Oberon*** BRH; KAL
  → Overture: mm. 11–16; pickup to 23–55; 117–145

TECHNICAL REQUIREMENTS

Please see "Technical Requirements" on p. 19 for important information regarding this section of the examination.

Studies/Etudes

Candidates should be prepared to play *one* selection from the following list. Each bulleted item (•) represents one selection for examination purposes.

Dont, Jacob
Etudes and Caprices, op. 35 SCH; INT
- **any *one***

Gaviniès, Pierre
24 Études (Matinées) PET; INT
- **any *one***

Kreutzer, Rodolphe
42 Études ou caprices INT
- ***one* of nos. 27–42**

Rode, Pierre
24 Caprices FIS; INT
- ***one* of nos. 4, 6, 7, 9, 11–24**

Technical Tests

Please see "Technical Tests" on p. 19 for important information regarding this section of the examination.

Scales, Arpeggios, and Double Stops

Please note that all scales, arpeggios, and double stops must be played from memory.

Scales	Keys	Range	Tempo	Bowing
Major Melodic minor Harmonic minor	all keys	3 octaves	♩ = 96	 (Galamian Pattern)
Artificial Harmonics Major Melodic minor Harmonic minor	A, B♭	2 octaves	♩ = 84	
Chromatic on	*any note*	3 octaves	♩ = 84	
Arpeggios				
Major Minor	all keys	3 octaves	♩. = 108	
Dominant 7th of	all major keys	3 octaves	♩ = 72	
Diminished 7th of	all minor keys			
Double Stops				
in 3rds, 6ths, 8ves Major Melodic minor Harmonic minor	E♭, E, F, F♯	2 octaves	♩ = 104	
in 8ves Major	E♭	1 octave solid fingered octaves alternate 1–3 and 2–4 fingerings on A and E strings	♩ = 104	
in 10ths Major	A	1 octave solid double stops on A and E strings		

EAR TESTS

Intervals

Candidates may choose to:

(a) sing or hum any of the following intervals after the examiner has played the first note *once*, OR

(b) identify any of the following intervals after the examiner has played the interval *once* in broken form.

– *above a given note*: any interval within the octave

– *below a given note*: any interval within the octave

Chords

Candidates will be asked to identify any of the following four-note chords after the examiner has played the chord *once* in solid form, close position:

- major and minor four-note chords in root position, first inversion, and second inversion. Candidates must identify the quality of the chord (major or minor) and name the inversion.
- dominant 7th and diminished 7th chords in root position.

Cadences

Candidates will be asked to identify, by name or by symbols, any of the following cadences when played in a simple phrase. The examiner will play the tonic chord *once* and then play the phrase *twice*. The phrase may be in a major or minor key and contain up to three cadences.

- perfect (authentic, V–I)
- plagal (IV–I)
- imperfect (I–V)
- deceptive (V–VI)

Melody Playback

Candidates will be asked to play back the *lower* part of a two-part phrase in any major key, either on the violin or on the piano. The examiner will name the key, play the tonic triad *once*, and play the phrase *twice*.

SIGHT READING

1. Candidates will be asked to play a composition approximately equal in difficulty to repertoire of a Grade 8 level.
2. Candidates will be asked to clap or tap the rhythm of a melody in $\frac{2}{4}$ or $\frac{3}{4}$ time. A steady pace and rhythmic accentuation is expected.

THEORY CO-REQUISITES

Grade 2 Rudiments
Grade 3 History
Grade 4 Harmony *or* Grade 4 Keyboard Harmony
Grade 4 History

Performer's ARCT

THE ARCT EXAMINATION

Please see "Theory Examinations: Prerequisites and Co-requisites" on p. 7, "ARCT Examinations" on p. 8, "Classification of Marks" on p. 15, and "Supplemental Examinations" on p. 16 for important details regarding the application for an ARCT examination. Candidates are strongly recommended to study for at least two years after passing the Grade 10 examination.

The ARCT diploma is the culmination of the RCM Examinations Certificate Program. The Performer's ARCT examination will be evaluated as a concert performance. Excellence in every aspect of performance is expected. Candidates must achieve an Honours standing (70 percent) in order to be awarded an ARCT diploma.

Policy Regarding Pass and Failure

If a candidate is able to preserve the continuity of a performance of a work despite a small break in concentration, a passing mark will not be precluded.

The candidate's performance of a work may receive a failing grade for any of the following reasons:

- lack of stylistic awareness
- repeated interruptions in the continuity
- substantial omissions
- textual inaccuracies
- complete breakdown of the performance

Marking Criteria

First Class Honours with Distinction: 90–100
Only truly exceptional candidates achieve this category. Candidates must demonstrate complete technical command and perform with a confident, masterful style. These candidates clearly demonstrate an authentic personal performance spark.

First Class Honours: 85–89
Candidates present a truly engaging and intelligent performance, displaying technical polish and finesse, definite and apt characterization, and a sense of spontaneity.

First Class Honours: 80–84
Candidates are technically solid and demonstrate sensitivity, intelligence, and talent. They are well prepared and able to execute the examination requirements thoughtfully and confidently.

Honours: 70–79
Candidates exhibit thorough and careful preparation and demonstrate some interpretive skills. Repertoire is presented with overall command and accuracy. There is awareness and general security in technical elements.

REPERTOIRE

Please see "Examination Repertoire" on pp. 12–13 for important information regarding this section of the examination.

Candidates should be prepared to play *four* contrasting selections: one from List A, one from List B, one from List C, and one from List D.

- List A includes concertos.
- List B includes sonatas.
- List C includes concert pieces.
- List D includes unaccompanied works.

Each bulleted item (•) represents one selection for examination purposes. Unless otherwise indicated, candidates should prepare the complete work. Please note that the selections in List B need not be memorized.

The length of the performance must be between 40 and 50 minutes. The examiner may stop the performance if it exceeds the allotted time.

LIST A

Barber, Samuel
- **Concerto**, op. 14 SCH
  → 1st *and* 2nd movements, with cadenza

Beethoven, Ludwig van
- **Concerto in D major**, op. 61 HEN; PET; INT
  → 1st *and* 2nd movements, with cadenza

Bruch, Max
- **Concerto in D minor**, op. 44 FIS
  → 1st *and* 2nd movements, with cadenza
- **Scottish Fantasy**, op. 46 SCH; INT
  → 1st *and* 2nd movements *OR* 3rd *and* 4th movements

Conus, Jules
- **Concerto in E minor** FIS; MAS; INT
  → 1st *and* 2nd movements

Dvořák, Antonín
- **Concerto in A minor**, op. 53 INT
  → 1st *and* 2nd movements *OR* 3rd *and* 4th movements

Elgar, Edward
- **Concerto in B minor** MAS
  → 1st *and* 2nd movements

Glazunov, Alexander
- **Concerto in A minor**, op. 82 INT
  → 1st movement *and* 2nd movement to the *Allegro*

Lalo, Edouard
- **Symphonie espagnole**, op. 21 SCH
  → 1st *and* 4th movements *OR* 4th *and* 5th movements

Mendelssohn, Felix
- **Concerto in E minor**, op. 64 FIS; PET
  → 1st *and* 2nd movements

Mozart, Wolfgang Amadeus
- **Concerto in A major**, K 219 INT
  → 1st *and* 2nd movements, with Joachim's cadenzas

Paganini, Niccolò
- **Concerto no. 1 in D major**, op. 6 SIM; INT
  → 1st *and* 2nd movements

Prokofiev, Sergei
- **Concerto no. 1 in D major**, op. 19 INT
  → 1st *and* 2nd movements
- **Concerto no. 1 in G minor**, op. 63 INT
  → 1st *and* 2nd movements

Saint-Saëns, Camille
- **Concerto in B minor**, op. 61 SCH; INT
  → 1st *and* 2nd movements

Vieuxtemps, Henri
- **Concerto no. 4 in D minor**, op. 31 FIS; INT
  → 1st *and* 2nd movements
- **Concerto no. 5 in A minor**, op. 37 PET; INT
  → 1st *and* 2nd movements

Weinzweig, John
- **Concerto** CMC
  → 1st *and* 2nd movements

Wieniawski, Henryk
- **Concerto in D minor**, op. 22 PET; INT
  → 1st *and* 2nd movements

LIST B

Adaskin, Murray
- **Sonata** (1946) CMC
  → 1st *and* 2nd movements

Beethoven, Ludwig van
- **Sonata in C minor**, op. 30, no. 2 HEN
  → *two* contrasting movements
- **Sonata in A major** ("Kreutzer"), op. 47 HEN
  → *two* contrasting movements

Brahms, Johannes
- **Sonata in D minor**, op. 108 BAR; INT
  → *two* contrasting movements

Coulthard, Jean
- **Duo Sonata** BER

Debussy, Claude
- **Sonata in G minor** DUR; PET
  → *two* contrasting movements

Dolin, Samuel
- **Sonata** BER
  → *two* contrasting movements

Fauré, Gabriel
- **Sonata in A major** HEN; SCH; INT
  → *two* contrasting movements

Franck, César
- **Sonata in A major** HEN, SCH
  → *two* contrasting movements

Grieg, Edvard
- **Sonata in G major**, op. 13 PET; FIS
  → 1st *and* 2nd movements

Hindemith, Paul
- **Sonata in D major**, op. 11, no. 2 OTT
  → 1st *and* 2nd movements

Morawetz, Oskar
- **Duo** RIC
- **Sonata no. 1** (1956) AEN; CMC

Mozart, Wolfgang Amadeus
- **Sonata in B flat major**, K 454 HEN

Prokofiev, Sergei
- **Sonata in D**, op. 94a INT
  → *two* contrasting movements

Raum, Elizabeth
- **Sonata** CMC

Respighi, Ottorino
- **Sonata in B minor** RIC
  → *two* contrasting movements

Somers, Harry
- **Sonata no. 2** BER
  → *two* contrasting movements

Strauss, Richard
- **Sonata in E flat major**, op. 18 UNI
  → *two* contrasting movements

Stravinsky, Igor
- **Duo concertante** B&H
  → *two* contrasting movements

Tartini, Giuseppe
- **Sonata in G minor**, op. 1, no. 10 ("Devil's Trill") FOL; INT
  → *two* contrasting movements, with cadenza

Weinzweig, John
- **Sonata** OUP

LIST C

Andrzejowski, Uminska
- **Burleska** PWM

Bartók, Béla
- **Rhapsody no. 1** B&H

Bazzini, Antonio
- **Ronde des lutins**, op. 25 INT

Chausson, Ernest
- **Poème**, op. 25 INT; PET

Eckhardt-Gramatté, Sophie-Carmen
Ten Caprices CMC
- ***one* of nos. 5–10**

Falla, Manuel de
- **Dance espagnole** (arr. Fritz Kreisler from *La vida breve* FIS)

Hétu, Jacques
- **Rondo varié pour violon seul**, op. 25 DOM

Kreisler, Fritz
- **Caprice viennois** FOL
- **Recitative and Scherzo caprice** FOL
- **Tambourin chinois** FOL

Paganini, Niccolò
Twenty-Four Caprices, op. 1 EMB
- ***one* caprice**

Papineau-Couture, Jean
- **Trois caprices** PER
  → *two* contrasting movements

Pentland, Barbara
- **Vista** BER

Prévost, André
- **Improvisation I pour violon seul** DOM

Raum, Elizabeth
- **Les ombres** CMC

Ravel, Maurice
- **Tzigane** DUR

Saint-Saëns, Camille
- **Havanaise**, op. 83 FIS; SCH; INT
- **Introduction and Rondo capriccioso**, op. 28 FIS; SCH; INT

Sarasate, Pablo de
- **Habañera** (*Spanish Dance,* op. 21, no. 2) INT
- **Introduction and Tarantelle**, op. 43 INT
- **Zapateado** (*Spanish Dance,* op. 23, no. 2) INT; EMB
- **Zigeunerweisen**, op. 20 FIS; INT

Stravinsky, Igor
- **Suite italienne** B&H
  → 1st, 3rd, *and* 6th movements

Szymanowski, Karol
- **La fontaine d'Aréthuse**, op. 30, no. 1 PWM

Tchaikovsky, Pyotr Il'yich
- **Waltz-Scherzo**, op. 34 INT

Vaughan Williams, Ralph
- **The Lark Ascending** OUP

Wieniawski, Henryk
- **Polonaise brillante in A major**, op. 21 INT; SCH
- **Polonaise in D major**, op. 4 INT
- **Scherzo tarantella in G minor**, op. 16 PET; FIS
- **Souvenir de Moscou** ("Airs russes"), op. 6 FIS

Ysaÿe, Eugène
Six Sonatas, op. 27 SCH
- **Sonata no. 1**
  → *two* contrasting movements
- **Sonata no. 2**
  → *two* contrasting movements
- **Sonata no. 3**
  → complete
- **Sonata no. 4**
  → *two* contrasting movements
- **Sonata no. 5**
  → complete
- **Sonata no. 6**
  → complete

Zarzycki, Aleksander
- **Mazurka in G major**, op. 26 PWM
- **Mazurka in E major**, op. 39 PWM

LIST D

Bach, Johann Sebastian
- **Partita no. 2 in D minor**, BWV 1004 BAR; HEN
  → Chaconne
- **Sonata no. 1 in G minor**, BWV 1001 BAR; HEN
  → Fugue

Bach, Johann Sebastian (continued)
- **Sonata no. 2 in A minor**, BWV 1003 BAR; HEN
  → Fugue
- **Sonata no. 3 in C major**, BWV 1005 BAR; HEN
  → Fugue

ORCHESTRAL EXCERPTS

Candidates should be prepared to play *two* excerpts: one from List 1 (orchestral tutti parts), and one from List 2 (excerpts that include a concertmaster solo). Candidates should prepare the first violin part. In addition, candidates are encouraged to listen to and be familiar with the works from which these excerpts are taken.

- All orchestral excerpts are included in *Violin Series, Third Edition: Orchestral Excerpts* (Mississauga, Ontario: Frederick Harris Music, 2006).
- Alternatively, candidates may use standard published orchestral parts for the specific excerpts. The listings below include measure numbers and a suggested publisher for each excerpt.

LIST 1: Orchestral Tutti Parts

Mendelssohn, Felix
- **Incidental Music to *A Midsummer Night's Dream***
  → I. *Scherzo*: mm. 17–99; 115–135; 237–250; 274 to end

Prokofiev, Sergei
- **Symphony No. 1** ("Classical")
  → 1st movement: mm. 1–32 (beat 1)
  → 4th movement: mm. 1–41; 129–169 (beat 1); 213 to end

Schumann, Robert
- **Symphony No. 2 in C major**, op. 61
  → 2nd movement (*Scherzo*): mm. 1–96; 360 to end

Smetana, Bedřich
- ***The Bartered Bride***
  → Overture: mm. 1–14; 31–66; 128–170; 401–421

Strauss, Richard
- **Don Juan**, op. 20
  → mm. 1–62; 165–195; 367–424

LIST 2: Excerpts that include a Concertmaster Solo

Beethoven, Ludwig van
- **Missa solemnis**, op. 123
  → Sanctus (Benedictus): mm. 110–234

Rimsky-Korsakov, Nicolai Andreyevich
- **Capriccio espagnol**, op. 34
  → 1st movement *(Alborada)*: mm. 55–72
  → 3rd movement *(Alborada)*: mm. 14–27; 41–63
  → 4th movement *(Scena e canto gitano)*: solo cadenza
  → 5th movement *(Fandango asturiano)*: mm. 25–36; 51–61
- **Schéhérazade**, op. 35
  → 1st movement: mm. 14–18; 94–102 (beat 1)
  → 2nd movement: mm. 14–18
  → 3rd movement: mm. 142–165
  → 4th movement: mm. 8–9; 29–30 (cadenza), 641–665

Strauss, Richard
- **Ein Heldenleben**
  → mm. 191–284; 311–335

Tchaikovsky, Pyotr Il'yich
- **Swan Lake Suite**
  → 4th movement *(Scène)*: mm. 10–34; 42–57; pickup to 66–72; pickup to 79–107

THEORY PREREQUISITES

Grade 2 Rudiments
Grade 3 History
Grade 4 Harmony *or* Grade 4 Keyboard Harmony
Grade 4 History

THEORY CO-REQUISITES

Grade 4 Counterpoint
Grade 5 Harmony and Counterpoint *or* Grade 5 Keyboard Harmony
Grade 5 History
Grade 5 Analysis

PIANO CO-REQUISITE

Grade 6 Piano

Teacher's ARCT

The Teacher's ARCT will be awarded only to candidates eighteen years of age or older.

Please see "Theory Examinations: Prerequisites and Co-requisites" on p. 7, "ARCT Examinations" on p. 8, "Classification of Marks" on p. 15, and "Supplemental Examinations" on p. 16 for important details regarding the application for an ARCT examination. Candidates are strongly recommended to study for at least two years after passing the Grade 10 examination and to have at least one year of teaching experience.

TEACHER'S ARCT PART 1: Performance of Repertoire, Orchestral Excerpts, Technical Requirements, Ear Tests, and Sight Reading

REPERTOIRE

Please see "Examination Repertoire" on pp. 12–13 for important information regarding this section of the examination.

Candidates should prepare *three* selections:

- one from the repertoire listed for Grade 9
- one from the repertoire listed for Grade 10
- one from the repertoire listed for the Performer's ARCT

The program must include:

- a concerto (first movement only)
- a sonata (two contrasting movements)
- a concert piece

Candidates are encouraged to choose a program that includes contrasting musical styles, periods, and keys.

Orchestral Excerpts

Candidates should be prepared to play *two* excerpts from those listed for the Performer's ARCT examination: one from List 1 (orchestral tutti parts), and one from List 2 (excerpts which include a concertmaster solo). Please note that orchestral excerpts need not be memorized. All orchestral excerpts are included in *Violin Series, Third Edition: Orchestral Excerpts* (Mississauga, Ontario: Frederick Harris Music, 2006).

TECHNICAL REQUIREMENTS

Please see "Technical Requirements" on p. 19 for important information regarding this section of the examination.

Studies/Etudes

No studies/etudes are required for the Teacher's ARCT.

Scales, Arpeggios, and Double Stops

Candidates should be prepared to play the scales, arpeggios, and double stops as listed for the Grade 10 examination. Please note that scales, arpeggios, and double stops must be memorized.

EAR TESTS

Metre

Candidates will be asked to identify the time signatures of four-measure passages. The examiner will play each passage once.

– *time signatures*: 2/4, 3/4, 6/8, 9/8

Intervals

Candidates may choose to:
(a) sing or hum the intervals listed below after the examiner has played the first note *once*, OR
(b) identify the intervals listed below after the examiner has played the interval *once* in broken form.

– *above a given note*: any interval within a major 9th
– *below a given note*: any interval within an octave

Chords

Candidates will be asked to identify, by chord symbols or names (I, tonic, V, dominant, etc.), the chords used in a four-measure phrase in a major key. The phrase will begin with a tonic chord and may include chords on the first, second, fourth, fifth, and sixth degrees of the scale. The final cadence may contain a cadential six-four chord and/or a dominant 7th chord.

The examiner will play the tonic chord *once* and then play the phrase *twice* in a slow to moderate tempo. During the second playing, the candidate will name each chord after it has been played by the examiner.

Melody Playback

Candidates will be asked to play back *both* parts of a two-part phrase in a major key together, either on the violin or on the piano. The examiner will name the key, play the tonic triad *once*, and play the phrase *twice*.

SIGHT READING

1. Candidates will be asked to play a given passage approximately equal in difficulty to repertoire of a Grade 9 level.
2. Candidates will be asked to play a passage equal in difficulty to repertoire of a Grade 5 level, demonstrating the musical features and characteristics of the piece.
3. Candidates will be asked to clap or tap the rhythm of a melody. A steady pace and rhythmic accentuation are expected.

TEACHER'S ARCT PART 2: *Viva Voce* Examination

A: Pedagogical Principles

This part of the examination will test the candidate's knowledge of the principles of violin playing including:
- the construction of the violin
- the position and action of the fingers, hands, and arms
- the production of tone
- technical tools (such as exercises, studies/etudes, scales, and arpeggios) necessary for the development of intonation, shifting, bowings, and tone quality

B: Applied Pedagogy

Teaching Repertoire

Candidates should select a group of eighteen pieces from *Violin Syllabus, 2006 edition* repertoire lists (three pieces for each of Grades 3 through 8). The works chosen from each grade should constitute a well-balanced group.

A list of the repertoire must be given to the examiner.

Candidates will be asked to perform a selection of these works and discuss teaching problems that may be encountered, including details of style and interpretation. (Please note that these pieces need not be memorized, but the performance should be at an honours level for the grade.)

Demonstration Lesson

The examiner will select and perform one work from the candidate's list of teaching repertoire. The candidate will be expected to detect errors in the examiner's performance (notation, time values, rhythm, phrasing, interpretation, etc.), demonstrate corrections, and suggest practice strategies to address the problems.

TEACHER'S ARCT PART 3: Teacher's ARCT Written Examination

Examination length: 3 hours
Passing mark: 70 percent
Candidates should be prepared to discuss the following topics:
- issues likely to arise in teaching intonation, rhythm, tone, shifting, bowing, articulations, phrasing, style and interpretation, memorization, sight reading, and ear training
- knowledge of the history of the violin and performance practice for music of the Baroque, Classical, and Romantic eras
- solutions for common technical problems
- suitable teaching material for all levels, from beginner up to and including Grade 8
- ways in which a teacher may help a student to develop confidence and concentration

Candidates may be asked to add editorial markings to a short passage of violin music, including articulations, dynamics, phrasing, expression marks, Italian terms, and fingerings. The title and tempo of the composition will be given. Candidates may also be asked to write several short exercises designed to correct common technical problems encountered by violin students.

For a reading list and reference material, please see "Bibliography" on pp. 75–78.

THEORY PREREQUISITES

Grade 2 Rudiments
Grade 3 History
Grade 4 Harmony *or* Grade 4 Keyboard Harmony
Grade 4 History

THEORY CO-REQUISITES

Grade 4 Counterpoint
Grade 5 Harmony and Counterpoint *or* Grade 5 Keyboard Harmony
Grade 5 History
Grade 5 Analysis

PIANO CO-REQUISITE

Grade 8 Piano

Section 4 – Theory Examinations

Theory examinations are given in the subjects listed below. Please refer to the current RCM *Theory Syllabus* for detailed information on theory examinations and recommended textbooks.

All theory co-requisites must be completed before or within five years after the respective session of the practical examination to which they apply. Extensions will not be granted. Candidates are strongly advised to complete their theoretical work before, or at the same time as, their practical examination. (Please see p. 8 for a list of theory prerequisites and co-requisites.)

RUDIMENTS

Preliminary Rudiments
Elements of music for the beginner.
– One-hour examination.

Grade 1 Rudiments
A continuation of Preliminary Rudiments for students with more music reading experience.
– Two-hour examination.

Grade 2 Rudiments
Preliminary and Grade 1 Rudiments with the addition of foundation material necessary to the study of harmony.
– Two-hour examination.

HARMONY, KEYBOARD HARMONY, COUNTERPOINT, AND ANALYSIS

Introductory Harmony
A continuation of Grade 2 Rudiments with the introduction of elementary four-part writing and melodic composition in major keys, chord symbols, and non-chord tones.
– Three-hour examination.

Grade 3 Harmony
The fundamentals of four-part writing in major keys; melodic composition; harmonic and structural analysis in major and minor keys. Familiarity with material of Grade 2 Rudiments is strongly advised.
– Three-hour examination.

Grade 3 Keyboard Harmony
The material of Grade 3 Harmony at the keyboard. This examination may be substituted for Grade 3 Harmony in fulfilment of certificate requirements.

Grade 4 Harmony
Intermediate four-part writing and melodic composition in major and minor keys; modulation; harmonic and structural analysis; musical forms. Completion of Grade 3 Harmony is strongly advised.
– Three-hour examination.

Grade 4 Keyboard Harmony
The material of Grade 4 Harmony at the keyboard. This examination may be substituted for Grade 4 Harmony in fulfilment of certificate requirements.

Grade 4 Counterpoint
Simple two-part counterpoint in Baroque style; invertible counterpoint at the octave and the 15th. Completion of Grades 3 and 4 Harmony is strongly advised.
– Three-hour examination.

Grade 5 Harmony and Counterpoint
Advanced harmonic and intermediate contrapuntal techniques (for two voices). Completion of Grades 3 and 4 Harmony and Grade 4 Counterpoint is strongly advised.
– Three-hour examination.

Grade 5 Keyboard Harmony
The material of Grade 5 Harmony and Counterpoint at the keyboard. This examination may be substituted for Grade 5 Harmony and Counterpoint in fulfilment of certificate requirements.

Grade 5 Analysis
Advanced harmonic and structural analysis of musical forms based on the material of Grades 3 and 4 Harmony, and Grade 5 Harmony and Counterpoint, as well as short post-1900 compositions.
– Three-hour examination.

MUSIC HISTORY

Grade 3 History

An overview of styles, composers, and music of the Baroque, Classical, and Romantic periods, and the 20th century.
– Three-hour examination.

Grade 4 History

Music of the Medieval, Renaissance, Baroque, and Classical periods, with emphasis on the development of musical genres and forms.
– Three-hour examination.

Grade 5 History

Styles, composers, and music of the 19th, 20th, and 21st centuries, including Canadian music.
– Three-hour examination.

MUSICIANSHIP

At the option of candidates, these examinations may be substituted for the Ear Tests requirements for Grades 8 to 10 and ARCT practical examinations.

Junior Musicianship

Singing and/or identification of scales, intervals, and chords; aural analysis of simple harmonic progressions; singing back and sight singing of simple rhythms and melodies. To be used with Grade 8 practical examinations.

Intermediate Musicianship

Singing and/or identification of scales, intervals, and chords; aural analysis of harmonic progressions; singing back and sight singing of rhythms and melodies. To be used with Grade 9 practical examinations.

Senior Musicianship

Singing and/or identification of scales, intervals, and chords; aural analysis of harmonic progressions to the Grade 4 Harmony level; singing back and sight singing of rhythms and melodies. To be used with Grade 10 practical examinations and/or ARCT; the minimum acceptable mark is 70 percent.

CLASSIFICATION OF THEORY MARKS

First Class Honours with Distinction	90–100
First Class Honours	80–89
Honours	70–79
Pass	60–69

Section 5 – Bibliography

The following texts are useful for reference, teaching, and examination preparation. No single text is necessarily complete for examination purposes.

GENERAL RESOURCES

Sight Reading and Ear Training

Bennett, Elsie, and Hilda Capp. *Sight Reading and Ear Tests.* 10 vols. Mississauga, Ontario: Frederick Harris Music, 1968–1970.

Berlin, Boris, and Andrew Markow. *Ear Training for Practical Examinations: Melody Playback/Singback.* 4 vols. (Levels 1 to ARCT). Mississauga, Ontario: Frederick Harris Music, 1986–1988.

———. *Ear Training for Practical Examinations: Rhythm Clapback/Singback.* 3 vols. (Levels 1 to 7). Mississauga, Ontario: Frederick Harris Music, 1989–1991.

———. *Four Star Sight Reading and Ear Tests.* Ed. Scott McBride Smith. 11 vols. Rev. ed. (Introductory to Level 10). Mississauga, Ontario: Frederick Harris Music, 2002.

Berlin, Boris, and Warren Mould. *Basics of Ear Training.* (Levels 8 to ARCT). Miami, Florida: Warner Bros. Publications. First published Toronto: Gordon V. Thompson Music, 1968.

———. *Rhythmic Tests for Sight Reading.* (Levels 8 to ARCT). Miami, Florida: Warner Bros. Publications. First published Toronto: Gordon V. Thompson Music, 1969.

Harris, Paul. *Improve your Sight-reading! A Workbook for Examinations.* London: Faber Music, 1994.

Hindemith, Paul. *Elementary Training for Musicians.* 2nd ed. London: Schott & Co., 1974.

Official Examination Papers

Official Examination Papers. 15 vols. Mississauga, Ontario: Frederick Harris Music, published annually.

Preliminary Rudiments
Grade 1 Rudiments
Grade 2 Rudiments
Introductory Harmony
Grade 3 Harmony
Grade 3 Keyboard Harmony
Grade 3 History
Grade 4 Harmony
Grade 4 Keyboard Harmony
Grade 4 History
Grade 4 Counterpoint
Grade 5 Harmony and Counterpoint
Grade 5 Keyboard Harmony
Grade 5 History
Grade 5 Analysis

Individual ARCT Teacher's Written Examination papers are also available upon request.

General Reference Works

Donington, Robert. *The Interpretation of Early Music.* New rev. ed. London; Boston: Faber and Faber, 1989.

Burkholder, J. Peter, Donald Jay Grout, and Claude V. Palisca. *A History of Western Music.* 7th ed. New York: W.W. Norton, 2005.

Kallmann, Helmut, Gilles Potvin, and Kenneth Winters, eds. *Encyclopedia of Music in Canada.* 2nd ed. Toronto: University of Toronto Press, 1992 (available on-line at *www.thecanadianencyclopedia.com*).

Kamien, Roger. *Music: An Appreciation.* 8th ed. Boston: McGraw-Hill, 2004.

Latham, Alison, ed. *The Oxford Companion to Music.* Oxford: Oxford University Press, 2002.

Machlis, Joseph and Kristine Forney. *The Enjoyment of Music.* 9th ed. New York: W.W. Norton, 2003.

Marcuse, Sibyl. *Musical Instruments: A Comprehensive Dictionary.* New York: W.W. Norton, 1975.

Randel, Don Michael, ed. *The Harvard Biographical Dictionary of Music.* Cambridge, Massachusetts: Harvard University Press, 1996.

———. *The Harvard Dictionary of Music.* 4th ed. Cambridge, Massachusetts: Belknap Press of Harvard University Press, 2003.

Sadie, Stanley, ed. *The New Grove Dictionary of Musical Instruments.* 3 vols. London: Macmillan, 1993.

Sadie, Stanley, and John Tyrell, eds. The *New Grove Dictionary of Music and Musicians.* 2nd ed., 29 vols. London: Macmillan, 2001.

Slonimsky, Nicolas, and Laura Kuhn, eds. *Baker's Biographical Dictionary of Music and Musicians.* Centennial ed. 6 vols. New York: G. Schirmer, 2000.

Stolba, K. Marie. *The Development of Western Music: A History.* 3rd ed. Boston, Massachusetts: McGraw-Hill, 1998.

VIOLIN RESOURCES

Anthologies

Barber, Barbara, comp. and ed. *Solos for Young Violinists: Selections from the Student Repertoire.* 6 vols. Miami, Florida: Summy-Birchard, 1996.

Beckwith, John, arr. *Eight Miniatures from the Allen Ash Manuscript.* Mississauga, Ontario: Frederick Harris Music, 1993.

de Keyser, Paul, and Fanny Waterman, eds. *The Young Violinist's Repertoire.* 4 vols. London: Faber Music; New York: G. Schirmer, 1986.

Lenkei, Gabriella, ed. *Violin Music for Beginners.* Budapest: Editio Musica Budapest; London: Boosey & Hawkes, 1970.

Moffat, Alfred, ed. and arr. *Old Masters for Young Players.* 3 vols. Mainz: Schott, 1911, 1931, 1933; Boca Raton, Florida: Masters Music Publications, 1991.

Nelson, Sheila M. *Piece by Piece: Easy Graded Repertoire for Young Players* [violin and piano]. 2 vols. London; New York: Boosey & Hawkes, 1991.

——, ed. *Romantic Violinist.* London: Boosey & Hawkes, 1996.

Perlman, George, ed. *Violinists' First Solo Album.* New York: Carl Fischer, 1905.

Suzuki, Shin'ichi. *Suzuki Violin School.* 10 vols. Evanston, Illinois: Summy-Birchard, 1978.

Collections

Archer, Violet. *Twelve Miniatures for Violin and Piano.* Ed. Howard Leyton-Brown. Waterloo, Ontario: Waterloo Music, 1982.

Bach, Johann Sebastian. *Ten Little Classics for Violin and Piano.* Arr. Constance Seely-Brown. New York: Carl Fischer, 1917.

Bennett, Richard Rodney. *Up Bow, Down Bow.* London: Novello, 1979.

Carse, Adam. *Fiddle Fancies: Seven Short Pieces for Violin and Piano.* London: Stainer & Bell, 1921.

———. *The Fiddler's Nursery: For Violin and Piano.* London: Augener; USA: Broude Bros., 1923.

Colledge, Katherine and Hugh. *Waggon Wheels.* London; New York: Boosey & Hawkes, 1991.

———. *Fast Forward.* London: Boosey & Hawkes, 1992, 2002.

Coulthard, Jean, David Duke, and Jean Ethridge. *The Encore Series for Violin and Piano.* Ed. Katharine Rapoport. 6 vols. Mississauga, Ontario: Frederick Harris Music, 1995–1996.

———. *The Encore Series: Teacher's Manual.* Ed. Katharine Rapoport. 2 vols. Mississauga, Ontario: Frederick Harris Music, 1996.

de Keyser, Paul. *Violin Playtime: Very First Pieces with Piano Accompaniment.* 3 vols. London: Faber Music, 1986.

———. *Violin Playtime Studies: Really Easy Studies for the Young Violinist.* London: Faber Music, 1988.

Hyslop, Ricky. *Bow Ties: Advanced Solos for Violin.* Mississauga, Ontario: Frederick Harris Music, 1989.

———. *Music Stands: Easy Solos for Violin.* Mississauga, Ontario: Frederick Harris Music, 1987.

———. *String Knots: Intermediate Solos for Violin.* Mississauga, Ontario: Frederick Harris Music, 1988.

Jones, Edward Huws. *The Really Easy Violin Book: Very First Solos for Violin with Piano Accompaniment.* London: Faber Music, 1989.

Kabalevsky, Dmitri. *Albumstücke.* Frankfurt: Peters, 1964.

———. *Twenty Pieces for Violin and Piano,* op. 80. Toronto: Leeds, 1967; New York: Leeds, 1975.

Mackay, Neil. *Four Modern Dance Pieces.* London: Galliard, 1964.

Murray, Eleanor, and Phyllis Tate. *Tunes for My Violin.* London: Boosey & Hawkes, 1937.

Nelson, Sheila. *Moving Up: A First Set of Pieces in the Second Position.* London: Boosey & Hawkes, 1974.

———. *Moving Up Again: A First Set of Pieces in the Third Position.* London; New York: Boosey & Hawkes, 1987.

Norton, Christopher. *Microjazz for Starters: Twenty Graded Pieces in Popular Styles for Violin and Piano.* London: Boosey & Hawkes, 1990.

Pracht, Robert. *Twelve Easy Pieces,* op. 12. Boston: Boston Music, 1911.

Rose, Michael. *Fiddler's Ten: Easy Tunes for Violin with Piano.* London: Novello, 1978.

Shostakovich, Dmitri. *Albumstücke.* Ed. and arr. Konstantin Fortunatov. Frankfurt: Peters, 1967; Hamburg: Hans Sikorski, 2004.

Studies and Technique

Anderson, Gerald E. and Robert S. Frost. *All for Strings: A Comprehensive String Method.* 3 vols. San Diego, California: Neil A. Kjos, 1985.

Cohen, Mary. *Superstudies for Violin: Easy Original Studies for the Young Player.* 2 vols. London: Faber Music, 1993.

———. *Technique Flies High: 14 Advanced Studies for Solo Violin.* London: Faber Music, 1998.

———. *Technique Takes Off!: 14 Intermediate Studies for Solo Violin.* London: Faber Music, 1992.

Dont, Jacob, arr. Louis Svecenski. *Twenty-four Exercises,* op. 37. New York: G. Schirmer.

Geringas, Yaakov. *Shifting: Thirty Studies for Young Violinists.* Mississauga, Ontario: Frederick Harris Music, 1987.

Kayser, Heinrich Ernst. *Elementary and Progressive Studies for the Violin,* op. 20. New York: G. Schirmer, 1915.

Kinsey, Herbert. *Elementary and Progressive Studies for Violin.* 3 vols. London: Associated Board of the Royal Schools of Music, 1932–1941.

Kreutzer, Rodolphe, ed. Friedrich Hermann. *Forty-Two Études ou caprices.* London: Peters Edition Limited.

Mazas, Jacques-Féréol. *Seventy-five Melodious and Progressive Studies,* op. 36. New York: G. Schirmer.

Skelton, Robert. *The Complete Violin Technique Book.* Mississauga, Ontario: Frederick Harris Music, 1998.

Trott, Josephine. *Melodious Double-Stops.* 2 vols. New York: G. Schirmer, 1925, 1931.

Wohlfahrt, Franz. *Sixty Studies,* op. 45. Budapest: Editio Musica Budapest, 1962.

Orchestral Excerpts

Violin Series, Third Edition: Orchestral Excerpts. Mississauga, Ontario: Frederick Harris Music, 2006.

Bach, Johann Sebastian. *Violin Solos from the Sacred Cantatas, Masses, Passions and Oratorios.* Ed. Martin Wolfhurst. Kassel; New York: Bärenreiter, 1996.

Gingold, Josef, ed. *Orchestral Excerpts from the Symphonic Repertoire.* 3 vols. New York: International, 1953–1962.

Strauss, Richard. *Orchestral Excerpts from Symphonic Works: For Violin.* Ed. Prill. New York: International, 1944.

VIOLIN REFERENCE MATERIAL

Books

Auer, Leopold. *Violin Playing As I Teach It.* London: Gerald Duckworth, 1921, 1960, 1980.

Bachmann, Alberto A. *An Encyclopedia of the Violin.* New York: D. Appleton, 1929, 1937, 1975.

Boyden, David Dodge. *History of Violin Playing from its Origins to 1761.* London: Oxford University Press, 1965, 1975; Oxford: Clarendon Press, 1990.

Casals, Pablo. *Joys and Sorrows: Reflections of Pablo Casals as told to Albert E. Kahn.* New York: Simon & Schuster, 1970.

Fischer, Simon. *Basics, 300 Exercises & Practice Routines for the Violin.* London: Peters Edition Limited, 1997.

Flesch, Carl. *The Art of Violin Playing.* 2 vols. New York: Carl Fischer, 1924, 1930, 2000.

Galamian, Ivan. *Principles of Violin Playing and Teaching.* 3rd ed. Ann Arbor, Michigan: Shar Products, 1999.

Gerle, Robert. *The Art of Practising the Violin.* London: Stainer & Bell, Ltd., 1983, 1985.

Havas, Kató. *A New Approach to Violin Playing.* London: Bosworth, 1961, 1970.

———. *The Twelve Lesson Course in A New Approach to Violin Playing.* London: Bosworth, 1964.

Kolneder, Walter. *The Amadeus Book of the Violin: Construction, History, and Music.* Trans. and ed. Reinhard G. Pauly. Portland, Oregon: Amadeus Press, 1972, 1998.

Loft, Abram. *Violin and Keyboard: the Duo Repertoire: from the 17th Century to Mozart.* 2 vols. Portland, Oregon: Amadeus Press, 2003.

Menuhin, Yehudi. *Violin: Six Lessons with Yehudi Menuhin.* London: Faber Music, 1971, 1981.

Mozart, Leopold. *Treatise of the Fundamental Principles of Violin Playing.* Trans. Editha Knocker. 2nd ed. Oxford: Oxford University Press, 1951, 1985.

Pernecky, Jack M. *Teaching the Fundamentals of Violin Playing.* Ed. Lorraine Fink. Miami, Florida: Summy-Birchard Inc., 1998.

Rolland, Paul. *The Teaching of Action in String Playing.* Urbana, Illinois: Illinois String Research Associates, 1974, 2000.

Starr, William, ed. *The Suzuki Violinist.* Knoxville, Tennessee: Kingston Ellis Press, 1976.

Books continued

Stowell, Robin. *The Cambridge Companion to the Violin.* Cambridge: Cambridge University Press, 1992.

Szende, Ottó and Mihály Nemessuri. *The Physiology of Violin Playing.* London: Collet's, 1971.

Szigeti, Joseph. *Szigeti on the Violin.* London: Dover, 1969, 1979.

———. *A Violinist's Notebook.* London: Gerald Duckworth, 1964.

Yampolsky, I.M. *The Principles of Violin Fingering.* London: Oxford University Press, 1967, 1984.

Periodicals

American String Teacher
www.astaweb.com
American String Teachers Association
4153 Chain Bridge Road
Fairfax, Virginia USA 22030

American Suzuki Journal
Suzuki Association of the Americas
www.suzukiassociation.org
P.O. Box 17310
Boulder, Colorado USA 80308

Strad Magazine
www.thestrad.com
Orpheus Subscriptions Department
c/o WDIS Ltd.
Units 12 & 13
Cranleigh Gardens Industrial Estate
Southall, United Kingdom UB1 2DB

Strings Magazine
www.stringsmagazine.com
Strings
Box 469120
Escondido, California USA 92046

Associations and Websites

American String Teachers Association
www.astaweb.com

Suzuki Association of the Americas
www.suzukiassociation.org
P.O. Box 17310
Boulder, Colorado USA 80308

Sources of Violin Music

Royal Conservatory Music and Book Store
273 Bloor Street West
Toronto, Ontario M5S 1W2
tel: 416-585-2225
fax: 416-585-7801
toll-free: 1-866-585-2225

Canadian Music Centre
www.musiccentre.ca
20 St. Joseph Street
Toronto, Ontario M4Y 1J9
tel: 416-961-6601
fax: 416-961-7198

The Leading Note
www.leadingnote.com
370 Elgin St. Suite 2
Ottawa, Ontario K2P 1N1
tel: 613-569-7888

Shar Products Company
www.sharmusic.com
P.O. Box 1411
Ann Arbor, Michigan USA 48106
tel: 1-800-248-SHAR

The Soundpost
www.thesoundpost.com
93 Grenville Street
Toronto, Ontario M5S 1B4
tel: 416-971-6990
fax: 416-597-9923
toll-free: 1-800-363-1512

Steve Weiss Music
www.steveweissmusic.com
2324 Wyandotte Road
Willow Grove, Pennsylvania USA 19090
tel: 215-659-0100
fax: 215-659-1170
toll-free fax: 1-877-582-2494
(This on-line music service stocks more than 10,000 violin titles, including many items not available from general music stores.)

The Second Century

The curriculum and the examination system of The Royal Conservatory of Music are built on more than a century of commitment to the highest quality in the teaching and performing of music. Through the professional training program, the national examination system, and faculty of distinguished musicians, The Royal Conservatory of Music is recognized as the leading music-training force in Canada, and one of the most significant musical institutions in the Commonwealth.

The Royal Conservatory of Music (originally called the Toronto Conservatory of Music and incorporated in 1886) opened with an enrolment of 200 students and a staff of fifty teachers led by Edward Fisher. A decade later, when enrolment had grown to more than 1,000 students, the school moved to newly built facilities with a reception hall, offices, studios, classrooms, a lecture hall, and a concert hall. Additional studios, classrooms, and residences for out-of-town students were added over the next fifteen years. In 1898, the Conservatory established its first examination centres in several Ontario towns and opened branches in Toronto.

In 1913, following the death of Edward Fisher, Augustus Vogt, conductor of the Toronto Mendelssohn Choir, became Principal. Under Vogt's leadership, new programs were developed. The number of examination centres was increased, and enrolment continued to grow. By 1926 there were nearly 7,500 students and over 16,000 examination candidates. In association with Sir Edmund Walker, President of the Conservatory, Vogt established closer ties with the University of Toronto. In 1921, administration of operations passed to a Board of Trustees responsible to the University.

Ernest MacMillan (later Sir Ernest MacMillan) was named Principal in 1926. He implemented professional performance training programs, including the Artist Diploma Program and The Royal Conservatory Opera School. When MacMillan resigned in 1942, the leadership of the Conservatory passed briefly in turn to Norman Wilks and Charles Peaker. Ettore Mazzoleni served as Principal from 1945 to 1968.

In 1947, a Royal Charter was granted to the Conservatory by King George VI in recognition of its wide influence. The institution was renamed The Royal Conservatory of Music. During the four postwar decades, the Royal Conservatory of Music continued to develop under the leadership of distinguished musicians such as Boyd Neel, David Ouchterlony, Ezra Schabas, Gordon Kushner, and Robert Dodson.

In 1991, The Royal Conservatory of Music re-established its independence from the University of Toronto, and Dr. Peter Simon was named President of the newly independent school. Over the next few years with the strengthening of teaching programs, RCM Examinations was expanded and the range of RCM materials published by The Frederick Harris Music Co., Limited increased. In addition, two new areas of development were established. The first, a research arm called the RCM Centre for Learning, has as its objective the exploration of new ways to teach music. The second, the RCM Teacher Services, is an association designed to support and assist independent music teachers with services and educational opportunities.

Now in its second century, and in association with thousands of dedicated teachers across the country, The Royal Conservatory of Music assists in the education of more than a quarter of a million students annually. With a renewed commitment to excellence in music education and performance, with strengthened ties to its communities, and with the development of new teaching methods and materials, The Royal Conservatory of Music welcomes the opportunity to serve the needs of society in the 21st century.